SEVENTH WARD.

The

TRIBECA

COOKBOOK

A COLLECTION OF SEASONAL MENUS FROM NEW YORK'S
MOST RENOWNED RESTAURANT NEIGHBORHOOD

The

TRIBECA

COOKBOOK

PRESENTED, COMPILED, AND EDITED BY

MARY CLEAVER, JOY SIMMEN HAMBURGER, AND

MIMI SHANLEY TAFT

ILLUSTRATIONS BY ROBBIN GOURLEY

TEN SPEED PRESS
BERKELEY, CALIFORNIA

10

TEN SPEED PRESS
P.O. Box 7123
Berkeley, California 94707

Endpaper illustration: *Plan of the City of New York,* Drawn & Engraved for D. Longworth,
May 1808. Collection of The New-York Historical Society. Reproduced with permission.

Book design by Big Fish Books, San Francisco.

Library of Congress Cataloging-in-Publication Data

Cleaver, Mary.
   TheTriBeCa cookbook : seasonal menus from the chefs of New York's historic restau-
rant neighborhood / presented, compiled, and edited by Mary Cleaver, Mimi Shanley
Taft, and Joy Simmen Hamburger ; illustrations by Robbin Gourley.
       p.   cm.
   Includes index.
   ISBN 0-89815-634-3
   I. Entertaining. 2. Cookery. 3. Menus. 4. Restaurants—New York (N.Y.)
   I.Taft, Mimi. II. Hamburger, Joy Simmen. III. Title.
TX731.C587 1994
642'.4--dc20   94-20056
                                      CIP

Printed in Hong Kong

I   2   3   4   5 - 98   97   96   95   94

Acknowledgments

WE WOULD LIKE to thank all the chefs, proprietors, and staff members of Arqua, Barocco, Capsouto Frères, Chanterelle, The Cleaver Company, Duane Park Cafe, El Teddy's, Montrachet, Nosmo King, The Odeon, Tribeca Grill, and Two Eleven Restaurant—the twelve eating establishments featured—for the support, energy, and patience they provided during the writing of this book.

We would also like to thank most heartily our friends and family members for their enthusiasm for this project and for their tireless testing, tasting, and critiquing of recipes. We are especially grateful to Ashley, Annie, and Emma Hollister, Peter, Zoe, and Max Hamburger, and Lloyd, Daniel, Virginia, and Bennett Taft. Also to Annie Bosworth and Nick, Lukas, and Julia Pearson, who traveled home past midnight for three seasons of Saturday nights. A special thanks to Brian Banaszynski for his technical assistance.

Special thanks to all of the food purveyors whose ingredients were essential to the successful testing of each recipe, especially Frank Wilklow, Gourmet Garage, Katonah's Village Market, Sgaglio's Marketplace, Ridgefield Hay Day, Jefferson Market, Aux Delices des Bois, D'Artagnan, and The Cleaver Company.

Thanks also to Susan Ginsburg and the staff at Writer's House for their original and continued enthusiasm for this cookbook.

Thanks for the invaluable contribution made by our editors at Ten Speed Press, Kirsty Melville, Clancy Drake, and Robin Kelly. A final, special thanks to Robbin Gourley for her beautiful and inspired illustrations.

The

TRIBECA

COOKBOOK

CONTENTS

INTRODUCTION *10*

THE TRIBECA COOKBOOK PHILOSOPHY *12*

THE RESTAURANTS OF TRIBECA *14*

SPRING

BAROCCO
Warm Shrimp & Bean Salad *24*
Roast Rack of Lamb *26*
Roasted Potatoes with Fresh Sage & Rosemary *27*
Hazelnut & Almond Cake with Macerated
Berries & Whipped Cream *28*

CAPSOUTO FRÈRES
Smoked Salmon Rillettes *30*
Grilled Portobello Mushrooms with
Balsamic Vinaigrette *32*
Hazelnut-Crusted Fillet of Red Snapper with
Cardamom Bercy Sauce *33*
Strawberry Ginger Rhubarb Crisp *34*

THE CLEAVER COMPANY
A Spring Buffet
Asparagus, Morels, Ramps & Fiddlehead Ferns
with Orange Oil & Edible Flowers *36*
Pasta with Sautéed Greens & Roasted Garlic *38*
Grilled Chicken Salad with Thai Dressing *39*
Olive Breadsticks *40*
Savory Corn Madeleines *41*
Strawberry Bread Pudding *42*

NOSMO KING
Asparagus with Horseradish Vinaigrette
& Pickled Beets *43*
Pan-Fried Soft-Shell Crabs with Tomato
Vinaigrette & Fava Beans with Shallots &
Summer Savory *44*
Napoleon of Strawberries & Sweet Yogurt *47*

TRIBECA GRILL
A Four-Course Tasting Menu
Sauté of Foie Gras with Parsnips & Sweet
and Sour Cherries *48*
Paillard of Salmon in Fresh Laurier Vinaigrette
with Leeks, Tomatoes & Asparagus *49*
Squab with Young Morels, Roast Garlic
& Sage Polenta *52*
Warm Cashew *Financier* with Frozen Mascarpone
Mousse, Coffee Anglaise, Chocolate
Sauce & Candied Cashews *54*

TWO ELEVEN RESTAURANT
Portobello & Oyster Mushrooms
with Herbed Goats' Milk Cheese
in Puff Pastry *57*
Grilled Chicken Breast with Oregano
Butter, Warm Wild Rice Salad & Sautéed
Mustard Greens *58*
Orange Crème Brulée *61*

SUMMER

ARQUA
Saffron Risotto Cakes with Cheese &
Vegetable Relish 64
Vitello Tonnato 66
White Peaches with Proseco 67

CHANTERELLE
Salad of Maine Crab with Hearts of Palm 68
Sauté of Chicken with Parsley, Tomato & Garlic 69
Corn Custard 70
Plum *Clafouti* 71

DUANE PARK CAFE
Panzanella with Mixed Field Greens 73
Veal with Sweet Vermouth, Sage & Prosciutto 74
Potato Salad with Mushrooms &
Sun-Dried Tomatoes 75
White Peach Granita with Raspberries,
Zabaglione & Almond *Biscotti* 76

EL TEDDY'S
Mexican Buffet
Margaritas 78
Tostadas de Camarónes 78
Yucatán Grilled Steak, Chicken Breasts &
Whole Red Snapper 80
Pico de Gallo, Avocado Sauce & *Salsa Picante* 81
Arroz Verde 83
Torta de Tres Leches 83

MONTRACHET
Marinated Squid & Octopus Salad
with Sherry Vinaigrette, Mango &
Red Onion 85
Swordfish with Rosemary Polenta,
Tomatoes & Fresh Herbs 87
Plum *Financier* with Peach Purée 89

TRIBECA GRILL
Fresh Fava Bean & Asparagus
Soup 90
Sauté of Soft-Shell Crab with Wilted
Spinach & Warm Summer
Tomato Vinaigrette 91
Barbecued Breast of Duck with Sweet
Corn Succotash 92
Spiced Spoonbread 94
Orange Chiffon Cake with Lemon
Verbena Custard & Berry Compote 94

TWO ELEVEN RESTAURANT
Cold Curried Carrot Soup with
Cilantro 97
Broiled Salmon with Braised Escarole &
Fried Leek Garnish 98
Orzo with Lemon Thyme
Zucchini Broth 98
Chocolate Chunk Hazelnut Cake with
Raspberry Sauce & Whipped
Cream 100

FALL

THE CLEAVER COMPANY
A Cocktail Party
Cheese Straws 104
Moroccan Chicken Wrapped in Phyllo with a
Roasted Pepper Dipping Sauce 105
Cucumber Stars with Smoked
Salmon Cream 107
Endive with Roquefort & Walnuts 108
Oysters in Champagne Sauce 108
Blue Potatoes with Crème Fraîche
& Caviar 109
Ratatouille Tartlets 110
Tea-Smoked Shrimp Wrapped
in Spinach 111

DUANE PARK CAFE
Warm Goats' Milk Cheese in Phyllo with
Roasted Beets 112
Roasted Chicken with Oregano
Bruschetta Stuffing 114
Oven-Dried Tomatoes &
Whipped White Beans 115
Quince Fritters with Cider Caramel &
Walnut Brittle Ice Cream 116

EL TEDDY'S
Turban Squash & Ancho Chile Soup 118
Wild Mushroom & *Huitlacoche* Quesadillas
with Mixed Greens 120
Warm Apple Empanadas with Orange
Hibiscus Sauce 121

MONTRACHET
Grilled Quail Salad with Balsamic
Vinaigrette 123
Salmon with Lentils & Red Wine
Sauce 124
Hot & Cold Chocolate Truffle Torte
with Raspberry Purée 126

THE ODEON
Warm Chicory Salad with Sweet Garlic,
Croutons, Bacon & Roquefort Cheese 128
Grilled Striped Bass with Chanterelles
& *Haricots Verts* 130
Raspberry Almond Tart 131

WINTER

ARQUA
Pasta Fagioli 134
Sautéed Radicchio with Melted *Taleggio* &
Fontina Cheeses 135
Osso Buco with Saffron Risotto 136
Apple Tart 138

BAROCCO
Fennel & Parmigiano Salad 140
Fettucine with Rabbit, Squab
& Black Olives 140
Poached Pears with Zabaglione
Cream 143

The TRIBECA
COOKBOOK

CAPSOUTO FRÈRES
Nantucket Bay Scallops with Melted
Leeks & Basil *144*
Braised Sweetbreads with Madeira &
Wild Mushrooms *146*
Black Mission Fig Soufflés with
Walnut Crème Anglaise *148*

CHANTERELLE
Mussels with Lime & Basil *151*
Beef with Black Trumpet Mushrooms *151*
White Creamer Potato Pancakes with Herbs &
Goats' Milk Cheese *153*
Fallen Chocolate Soufflé Cake *154*

NOSMO KING
Roasted Sourdough Bread with Goats' Milk
Cheese, Red Peppers, Basil & Black
Olive Tapenade *156*
Seared Tuna with Spinach, White Beans
& Lime-Marjoram Vinaigrette *157*
Steamed Cranberry Pudding *158*

THE ODEON
Pan Roast of Oysters with Poblano
Chiles on Toasted Cornbread *160*
Grilled Lamb Shanks with Preserved Lemons
on Arugula *162*
Pear Turnovers *164*

BASICS AND TECHNIQUES *165*
SOURCES GUIDE *169*
INDEX *173*

INTRODUCTION

ALMOST TWO HUNDRED years ago, the area that New Yorkers now call TriBeCa was the location of this city's most important food distribution center, Washington Market. The area occupied about fifty-eight acres in a tight enclave of the southwestern tip of Manhattan and was bordered by Fulton Street to the south, Laight Street to the north, Hudson Street to the east, and the Hudson River to the west. Long ago, Washington Market's cobbled streets bustled with activity: ships docked along the Hudson, bringing goods from American and European food dealers; carts and trains hauled goods in and out of the area; and busy merchants sold fresh butter and eggs from the neighborhood's brick-and-cast-iron-fronted buildings. Nineteenth-century writer Thomas F. DeVoe wrote about Washington Market in *The Market Book*, published in 1862. In Devoe's words, the market was "without a doubt the greatest depot for the sale of all manner of edibles in the United States; it not only supplies many thousands of our citizens, but, I may say, many of the surrounding cities, towns, villages, hotels, steamers (both ocean and river) and shipping vessels of all description."

In 1912, New Yorkers celebrated the centennial of the founding of Washington Market. A local merchants' association published a historic program to mark the occasion. The program reported statistics that revealed just how busy Washington Market was in those early days:

Investigation shows that in their heavy season five railroads handling the bulk of the perishable foodstuffs at piers in this city receive in one day:

220 car loads of vegetables and potatoes
175 car loads of fruits and apples
60 car loads of berries
120 car loads of butter and eggs

At Washington Market the following quantity of goods were received annually:

73,000,000 pounds of butter
1,460,000,000 eggs
638,750,000 pounds of fruit
109,500,000 head of poultry and game
—*Official Souvenir: Centennial Celebration*, 1912

The march of time and the vision of urban planners brought changes to Washington Market. In 1968, the market was moved north to Hunts Point in the Bronx, where it remains today, and the once active community of old Washington Market fell silent, leaving large buildings with fading signs amid empty lots.

Historian Danny Lyon relates the events in *The Destruction of Manhattan* (1969): "The Washington Street Urban Renewal Project brought down twenty-four and a half blocks of mostly 19th century buildings on the west side of lower

Manhattan. Many of the buildings had been in continuous commercial use since before the Civil War." On a portion of this site, workers cleared buildings and erected the World Trade Center. Many hundreds of other buildings were abandoned and left vacant.

By 1977, the *New York Times* was reporting signs of new life in this ghost town that sported the name TriBeCa, "the unofficial name for the Triangle Below Canal Street." Artists, writers, actors, and other professionals in search of inexpensive housing were drawn to the old brick and cast-iron buildings, which lent themselves nicely to loft living. Gradually a new neighborhood began to emerge that today is host to a broad mix of growing families and professionals.

Following quickly on the heels of these new residents were young restaurateurs. The large ground floor spaces of the old warehouse buildings, with their high ceilings and open rooms, were ideal for restaurants, especially because rents were cheap in this relatively obscure neighborhood. In TriBeCa, young chefs were able to pursue their dreams of having their own New York restaurants by occupying the same spaces that had once housed cheese, coffee, and poultry exchanges. Thanks to the pioneering spirit of these restaurateurs, TriBeCa is once again a center for food. Within its borders are some of the city's—indeed some of the country's—finest

restaurants, offering superbly prepared fresh food from award-winning chefs who find their inspiration in traditional American cooking, the best of French and Italian fare, and original tastes all their own. In this cookbook we are proud to present a sampling from many of TriBeCa's finest restaurants in recipes geared for home chefs.

We feature twelve eating establishments, selected for their diversity and their longevity. The dishes they offer match our goal of presenting special, seasonal ingredients to inspire those who enjoy home entertaining. Keep in mind that this is not a guidebook or a critical restaurant review book; our decision to include or exclude a particular establishment does not reflect a judgment of any kind.

In addition to the restaurants featured in this book, there are many other fine restaurants in TriBeCa. We invite you to explore all of TriBeCa's restaurants and specialty food stores. Drop by the farmer's market held every Wednesday at N. Moore and Greenwich Streets and every Saturday on Greenwich in front of Washington Market Park. Many of the local restaurants purchase fresh fruits, vegetables, and flowers from this market, which is open almost all year round. Let this book be your introduction to TriBeCa. Discover on your own the creative spirit of this lively but sophisticated historic community.

THE TRIBECA COOKBOOK PHILOSOPHY

THIS COOKBOOK REFLECTS the philosophies of the chefs who create highly acclaimed meals in the TriBeCa area in downtown New York City. The common denominator for this diverse group is their use of high-quality, fresh, seasonal ingredients. To reflect this philosophy, we have arranged the recipes in this book according to season. Recipes in the Spring section, for example, call for young salad greens, asparagus, fiddlehead ferns, fresh strawberries, and other springtime foods. The primary ingredients in each recipe should be at their peak when you create the dish. As you become familiar with the dishes, you will be able to adapt some of the dishes to other seasons.

You may find that some ingredients are not readily available from the markets in your area. To help out, we have included a listing of purveyors who ship their products all over the country. Refer to the Sources Guide at the back of this book. Don't let hard-to-find ingredients prevent you from trying a dish. If you can't find an ingredient and don't want to send for it, consider a suitable substitution. That's what creative chefs do!

One ingredient that we do not recommend replacing, though, is fresh herbs. The flavors of meats and vegetables and other foods are greatly enhanced by the use of fresh herbs. Resist the temptation to use dried herbs in place of fresh ones. You'll be pleased with the results. To have a steady supply on hand, consider growing your own herbs. If this isn't practical, find local markets that carry fresh herbs in their produce section, or order them by mail from the merchants listed in the Sources Guide.

In recent years, supermarkets and specialty food stores across the country have begun to carry more and more food products, especially items that we used to consider "gourmet." A wide variety of interesting products are now available to consumers—both to home chefs and to restaurant patrons. As a result, tastes have changed, and so have expectations. The availability of high-quality, well-prepared foods has raised people's standards for excellence. As a home chef, you may feel the desire to be innovative, to use foods in new and different ways, and to offer high-quality cuisine to your guests. We have taken these factors into consideration in

developing this cookbook. The recipes will help you organize and pace yourself when planning to entertain at home. The instructions indicate what portions of a meal can be prepared in advance, and they suggest how to serve dishes for maximum effect of flavor and presentation. For additional suggestions, see the Basics and Techniques section toward the back of the book. This section also provides some recipes for stock and other prepared ingredients as well as some techniques for basic cooking procedures.

As a home chef, you will want to use this cookbook when you plan a special evening with family and friends. The menus are for small groups of four to eight people. They include appetizer, main course, and dessert. Of course,

not every special dinner is a candlelight affair. So we have included menus for a cocktail party, a tasting menu, casual suppers, and buffets.

The chefs have designed each menu to combine flavors that complement each other. Don't let this inhibit you from mixing and matching dishes throughout the book. In many cases, you can complement the main course dish with a simple green salad or a seasonal vegetable.

We had a terrific time testing these recipes, and we encourage you to have fun with this book. Each dish will be well worth the time and effort it takes to prepare. We hope that you will find some new favorite dishes to add to your repertoire for entertaining.

THE RESTAURANTS OF TRIBECA

The following profiles offer some insight into the personalities and inspirations of the chefs and owners of the twelve eating establishments featured in this book.

ARQUA

281 Church St.

CHEF LEO PULITO was born and raised in Arqua, a small town near Padua, in northeastern Italy. After studying cooking in Switzerland, Chef Pulito came to the United States. In the early 1980s he had his first introduction to the TriBeCa area. At that time he took charge of the kitchen at Ecco, an Italian restaurant on Chambers Street. Ecco drew a lively crowd from nearby City Hall and Wall Street. When the opportunity came to open his own restaurant, Chef Pulito chose to stay in lower Manhattan. He opened Arqua in 1987, naming the restaurant for his hometown in Italy.

When you enter Arqua you climb a short flight of stairs to an elegant high-ceilinged corner room wrapped by large windows. The hand-rubbed umber walls are gently washed by subtle lighting. A bar of pickled wood is vaguely reminiscent of weathered Renaissance buildings. A dramatic seasonal flower arrangement sits atop a pedestal in the center of the room.

Each year that he returns to Italy, Chef Pulito visits the chefs whose work he most admires, including the chefs at La Botta and La Montanella in Padua, and at Le Calandre in Arqua. While he cooks and exchanges ideas with the chefs, he finds inspiration for the dishes he serves at his own restaurant in New York. For this book, Chef Pulito has chosen variations on some classic Italian dishes.

BAROCCO

301 Church St.

FROM THE MOMENT it opened in June of 1986, Barocco has attracted people from the art, publishing, and design worlds. Conceived as a bistro-style Italian restaurant, Barocco offers simple and solid Tuscan fare that has received consistently high marks from reviewers over the years. Barocco is set in a spare high-ceilinged space accented by a black-and-white bar and adorned by an arrangement of fresh flowers. Light filters through glass block windows, masking its New York City urban location from diners. The restaurant feels like an Italian trattoria.

Chef Alessandro Prosperi was born in Florence, Italy. A self-taught chef, he earned his stripes at two New York restaurants—Word of Mouth and Carolina Restaurant—before opening

The
TRIBECA
COOKBOOK

Barocco with Daniel Emerman. Having grown up in Cleveland, Ohio, Mr. Emerman moved to Italy after college, where he developed his great love of Italian food.

In 1991, Mr. Emerman and Chef Prosperi expanded their business to include a specialty store, Barocco Alimentari, which sells prepared foods. Barocco Alimentari has two locations: one store is next to the restaurant in TriBeCa; the other is in Greenwich Village.

The simple high-quality food of Barocco is wonderful, whether you eat it at home or in the restaurant. The recipes that Mr. Emerman and Chef Prosperi have selected for this book are perfect examples of their unpretentious philosophy. Each menu is easy to prepare, full of flavor, and most rewarding for the home chef to present and for guests to savor.

CAPSOUTO FRÈRES

451 Washington St.
CAPSOUTO FRÈRES OPENED in 1980 and is one of the oldest restaurants in TriBeCa. The restaurant is owned by three brothers—Jacques, Samuel, and Albert Capsouto. They were born in Cairo, Egypt, and raised in Lyons, France. They moved to the United States in 1961. Together, they renovated the ground floor of the 1891 landmark neo-Flemish warehouse that now houses Capsouto Frères, transforming it into an elegant space with French doors that open onto a dining porch. In this setting, you can experience the

quintessential TriBeCa, savoring brunch under the umbrellas. There on the porch the energy of the busy New York streets contrasts the tranquility of the Hudson River view.

In 1986, Charles Tutino became the chef at Capsouto Frères. He had trained at La Côte Basque for six years. Chef Tutino brings to Capsouto Frères his philosophy of using fine, fresh, and seasonal ingredients, straightforward food design, and intelligent preparation. He is so thorough that he usually prepares ingredients that other restaurants often purchase, including jams, breads, pâtés, ice creams, and sorbets. His labor ensures a high standard of freshness and guarantees exceptional and original flavoring in all recipes, a quality reflected in the menus he selected to share in this book.

CHANTERELLE

2 Harrison St.
DAVID AND KAREN Waltuck opened the original Chanterelle Restaurant in 1979 in New York's Soho district. After ten years at that location they moved to a larger space in TriBeCa's landmark Mercantile Exchange building, which boasts one of the area's most striking facades. Chanterelle's dining room is noted for its architectural details, accented by Karen Waltuck's renowned floral arrangements. Rightly proud of their four-star rating from the *New York Times,* the Waltucks are committed to providing their diners with impeccable service. Karen Waltuck personally oversees the experience of the patrons.

Chef Waltuck became interested in cooking while attending City College in the early 1970s. After earning a degree in marine biology, he briefly attended the Culinary Institute of America. From there, he went on to La Petite Ferme, where he spent two years as luncheon chef.

In preparing his recipes, Chef Waltuck takes advantage of the best products available, seeking out small producers and suppliers of fresh seafood, produce, domestic and imported game, and, of course, wild mushrooms. His travels have influenced his style of cooking, which incorporates flavors from the Far East as well as Europe. He continually tries to refine his innovative cuisine, changing the menu monthly. His ceaseless energy has held him firmly in the forefront of his art.

Chanterelle is truly a collaborative effort between Chef Waltuck and Karen Waltuck. Prior to opening Chanterelle, Karen Waltuck worked in New York's fashion world as a coordinator and buyer for an East Side boutique. She specialized in European collections and traveled twice a year to France, Italy, and England on business. Her background contributes to her strong sense of style and her attention to detail. These skills, together with Chef Waltuck's sensational food and their combined energy, allow the Waltucks and Chanterelle to dazzle all who dine there. World-class sommelier Roger Dagorn has added his suggestions for pairing wines with the recipes Chef Waltuck has chosen to include in this book.

THE CLEAVER COMPANY

229 W. Broadway

THE CLEAVER COMPANY is a catering business and carry-out shop. Founded in 1978, it began as a small, one-woman business. Today, the company prepares intimate dinner parties as well as formal gatherings for thousands of people. It is renowned for its seasonally planned menus of elegant and healthful foods. In 1988, the Cleaver Company opened a retail shop in one of the oldest houses in TriBeCa, where devoted customers in the art, film, business, and publishing worlds line up for such delights as handmade scones, doughnuts, and brioches for breakfast; healthy salad samplers at lunch; and crispy herb roasted free-range chickens for dinner.

The team of cooks working at the Cleaver Company is headed by Elisa Sarno, a 1987 graduate of the New York Restaurant School. She joined the Cleaver Company in 1989. For seven years, Hillary Nelson, a 1986 graduate of the Culinary Institute of America, oversaw the growth of the Cleaver Company baking department, which includes a line of seasonal mail-order specialties, hand-painted cookies, and truffles. It is now run by baker Marie Regusis, who maintains the high standards that patrons have come to expect. The Cleaver Company bakers are also well known for their custom-designed birthday and wedding cakes.

The founder and president of the Cleaver Company is Mary Cleaver. During her company's early years, Chef Cleaver also worked as a corporate

chef, a pastry chef at J. S. Vandam, a food stylist, and a cooking teacher. For this book she has chosen to include two entertaining menus for larger groups: a spring buffet and a fall cocktail party. Both menus will allow you to experience some of the exceptional foods from which the Cleaver Company has earned its reputation.

DUANE PARK CAFE

157 Duane St.

THE BRIGHTLY PAINTED facade of Duane Park Cafe is accented with seasonal flowers and trees. It is an image that lends an air of Provence to Manhattan's gritty streets, enticing one to come inside and dine. Stepping though the doors, patrons are greeted by General Manager Alfred A. Chiodo and members of his warm and friendly staff who invite them to relax, linger, and fully enjoy the internationally inspired foods. A handsome dark wood bar surrounded by colorful stools provides an easy transition to the comfortable dining room beyond. The two spaces act as a metaphor for Chef Seiji Maeda's cooking philosophy: the bar is distinctly European in flavor and the dining room reflects the spare design of traditional Asian architecture.

Chef Maeda's background and influences are written in the foods he serves at Duane Park Cafe, which he founded in January of 1989. Born and raised in Japan, he moved to New York in the 1970s and graduated from the Culinary Institute of America in 1981. His post-graduate work took him from the Cajun kitchen of K-Paul's in New Orleans to the French cuisine served at the bistro Hubert's and the renowned Régine's, both in New York City. Chef Maeda combines the culinary influences of those restaurant kitchens with his own background. The results are dishes that defy ethnic categories. For this book he has included dishes that sound traditional. However, in preparing these recipes, home chefs will come to understand Chef Maeda's unique approach to combining ingredients that do not always culminate in traditional flavors.

EL TEDDY'S

219 W. Broadway

EL TEDDY'S IS located in one of the few spaces in TriBeCa that was a restaurant before the Washington Market was moved to Hunts Point. Formerly called Teddy's, it was a steak house that attracted a crowd of celebrities, including Liz Taylor, Richard Burton, and Jane Fonda. The new restaurant sports black-and-white photographs from this previous incarnation.

You can easily locate El Teddy's by the model of the Statue of Liberty's crown on the roof. This marker dates from another previous occupant, El Internationale, a tapas bar founded in the 1980s. Although the establishment was short-lived, it was highly regarded for its cuisine and for the star-studded clientele it attracted. Thus, El Teddy's takes its name from the two previous restaurants. Its decor is a brilliant mix of elements that trace the forty-year history of the space, with such whimsical additions as a sculpted awning made of cut glass and a maitre d' station that is encrusted with spherical marbles.

El Teddy's draws plenty of high-profile people to its tables, but food is the true star here. The triumvirate that creates El Teddy's fresh, innovative, Mexican-inspired food includes Chef Peter Klein, Sous-chef Ramiro Mendez, and Pastry Chef Judy Lyness. Chef Klein received his formal training at the Culinary Institute of America and gained professional experience at high-quality restaurants in New York, Florida, and California. In 1988, he became the executive chef of New York's China Grill, where for four years he honed his skills using exotic flavor combinations and unique presentations. He and Sous-chef Mendez worked together at the China Grill, where Mendez, as saucier, was in charge of over twenty different sauces and lunch service. Sous-chef Mendez came to New York from Puebla, Mexico. He brings both authenticity and innovation to El Teddy's menu. Pastry Chef Judy Lyness came to New York from Stowe, Vermont, where she had her own shop, Baker's Dozen. She joined El Teddy's kitchen after creating pastries exclusively for Henri Bendel on New York's Fifth Avenue. The wonderful desserts she shares with the *TriBeCa Cookbook* are ample evidence of her exceptional talents.

MONTRACHET

239 W. Broadway

MONTRACHET WAS OPENED in 1985 by Drew Neiporent, the restaurant entrepreneur who is also a founding owner of the Tribeca Grill. *New York Times* restaurant reviewer Ruth Reichl recently confirmed Montrachet's three-star rating. She wrote: "Montrachet has always had a style of its own, and each chef falls under the restaurant's spell. The food is refined yet aggressive. Its strength lies less in technique than in the quality of ingredients and the finesse with which they are combined." Montrachet's first chef, David Bouley, was succeeded by his sous-chef Debra Ponzek. Chris Gesualdi, her former sous-chef, currently heads the kitchen.

The cooking at Montrachet has been described as "modern French." While not typically classic, it is based in French technique. Many fresh herbs are used and sauces are light. The food shines at Montrachet, where the decor is low-key and the wine list exceptional. Montrachet is one of only four restaurants in the country that has received a four-star rating from the *Wine Spectator.* To achieve the total Montrachet effect, sommelier Daniel Johnnes has suggested some wines you can treat yourself to when savoring the Montrachet dishes at home.

The desserts at Montrachet are created by Pastry Chef David Blom, who began his career in his parents' Philadelphia-based bakery, where he started out as a pot scrubber. As the family business expanded, he worked his way up, eventually becoming a baker and cake decorator. Chef Blom attended the Culinary Institute of America, graduated in 1988, and began working at Montrachet as pastry chef in 1991. In March of 1994, he was named one of America's top ten pastry chefs by *Chocolatier* magazine. He has selected two of his favorite desserts to include in this book.

NOSMO KING

54 Varick St.

STEVE FRANKEL, PROPRIETOR, and Alan Harding, chef, rely on three guiding principles at their restaurant, Nosmo King. These are fine dining, fun dining, and healthful dining. Having provided for these three principles, they encourage diners to place the emphasis where they wish it.

Steve Frankel came to New York from Cleveland intending to open a restaurant. His first foray was Exterminator Chili, also located in TriBeCa. It served three grades of chili—Industrial, Residential, and Commercial—and quickly became a local hangout for the artists, writers, and musicians that live in the neighborhood. Having had his fill of slow-cooked meat and melted cheese, Mr. Frankel began to explore "cleaner" eating. He sought a place that offered the sophistication of fine dining combined with a cooking philosophy that reflected an awareness of organic foods. From this search evolved the ideas and guiding principles for Nosmo King.

After receiving his degree from the Culinary Institute of America and working at Rakel, Alan Harding joined Steve Frankel at Nosmo King. His cooking style features contemporary cuisine based on fresh, often organic ingredients. Chef Harding senses a growing concern among Americans about what they eat, where their food comes from, and how it is produced. He feels that "food should be enjoyed, not mistrusted."

Chef Harding's work at Nosmo King is only one expression of his commitment to social values, which is further reflected in his activities outside the restaurant. Chef Harding teaches inmates to cook through the Fresh Start Program on Riker's Island. He also teaches children about nutrition at the American Cancer Society and works with the Food and Hunger Hotline, an organization that feeds the homeless. Each of the recipes Chef Harding has chosen to include in this book will enable you to enjoy Nosmo King's philosophy of fine, fun, and healthful dining at home.

THE ODEON

145 W. Broadway

THE ODEON WAS founded in 1980 by Lynn Wagenknecht and Brian and Keith McNally. The Odeon was their inaugural effort in a series of restaurants they opened together or separately, all of which have achieved great success. The Odeon aspires to all of the best qualities of French brasseries and grand cafés that strive to provide worldly, urban folk with foods that can be enjoyed in an atmosphere that affords as little or as much formality as their moods require.

Chef Stephen Lyle was born in Paris to American parents. He spent his formative years in the south of France, where he began his cooking career in a separate kitchen his parents built for their five children. At age 17, he apprenticed in a small restaurant near Monte Carlo with a young and talented chef, where, in his own words, "the sauces were *à la minute* and the ingredients were not to be believed." In 1980, after working at the three-star French restaurant L'Oustaou de Baumanieres, Chef Lyle came to the United States and worked at La Tulipe and Le Plaisir; in 1984, he was made chef at Quatorze Bistro.

In 1989, Chef Lyle joined the Odeon with his assigned mission of overseeing the conversion of the existing menu to a bistro menu. Now, five years into this project, his cooking is still firmly grounded in French and Italian cooking, although he has also incorporated some ingredients of Mexican and Asian cuisine. His dishes have again made the Odeon one of the busiest restaurants in the city, with a broad clientele that includes artists, lawyers, and professionals from nearby Wall Street and City Hall as well as people from the fashion and entertainment industries. Such diners are a demanding bunch, with educated, discriminating palates. They are never disappointed at the Odeon.

TRIBECA GRILL

375 Greenwich St.

TRIBECA GRILL OFFERS a taste of Hollywood on the Hudson. Founded in 1990, it is owned by the Academy Award–winning actor Robert De Niro, noted restaurateur Drew Neiporent, and numerous other celebrities, including Bill Murray, Sean Penn, Christopher Walken, and Mikhail Baryshnikov. Occupying the ground floor of the old Martinson Coffee Warehouse, Tribeca Grill is a brick-walled square room punctuated by a grand mahogany bar and the artwork of Robert De Niro, Sr., the actor's father. The entertainment media regularly cover movie premieres and other high-profile events at Tribeca Grill (among them a visit from Nelson Mandela). But what keeps people coming back is the exceptionally high quality of food served night after night.

Chef Don Pintabona, a 1982 graduate of the Culinary Institute of America, has guided the culinary philosophy of Tribeca Grill from the beginning. After completing his formal training, Chef Pintabona traveled to Europe and worked with chefs George Blanc and Alain Derain of Restaurant George Blanc. From France he went to Osaka, Japan, where he worked as sous-chef under Chef M. Nishitani of Gentille Alouette. The influence of both these experiences is clearly expressed in the techniques and ingredients that Chef Pintabona favors in his dishes.

George McKirday has been the pastry chef at Tribeca Grill since it opened. He credits Michel

Fitoussi, formerly of Régine's, as his most important mentor. The elegant, rich desserts that Pastry Chef McKirday has included in this book will enable you to achieve professional results of the highest order at home.

TWO ELEVEN RESTAURANT

211 W. Broadway
PROPRIETOR KHALIL AYOUBI opened Two Eleven Restaurant in January 1981 when, according to local tradespeople, "you could fire a cannon from Canal Street to the Trade Towers and not hit anyone." Mr. Ayoubi believed in the future of TriBeCa and was inspired by the sixteen foot ceilings and floor-to-ceiling windows of the former furniture showroom his restaurant now occupies. Over the years he has refined the architectural details of the space, converting the former truck loading dock into one of TriBeCa's loveliest terraces for outdoor eating.

Guy Cerina joined Two Eleven Restaurant as chef in June, 1993. His position gives him the opportunity to create seasonal menus that reflect his cooking philosophies. Chef Cerina comes from a family deeply rooted in the restaurant business. His grandfather owned and operated a restaurant in Hampton Bays, Long Island, called the Canoe Place Inn. The establishment boasted a ballroom, living quarters for the staff, and, most importantly, a farm that grew much of the produce served in the restaurant. Chef Cerina's uncle, Franco Caselli, has served many years in New York City's restaurant business and gave Chef Cerina his start at L'Escargot Restaurant on West 55th Street in Manhattan. After working at the restaurant for two years, Chef Cerina attended the Culinary Institute of America, graduating in 1986. Since then he has worked at some of New York City's finest and busiest restaurants—Tavern on the Green, Maxim's, Sign of the Dove, and Café des Artistes. Having accumulated an impressive résumé, Chef Cerina is excitedly pursuing his career at Two Eleven Restaurant. He has selected recipes for this cookbook that are strong examples of his unique abilities to combine fresh flavor with dishes that are easy to prepare.

Spring

BAROCCO

Spring Menu

❧

WARM SHRIMP
& BEAN SALAD

ROAST RACK
OF LAMB

ROASTED
POTATOES
WITH FRESH
SAGE &
ROSEMARY

HAZELNUT &
ALMOND CAKE
WITH MACERATED
BERRIES
& WHIPPED CREAM

WARM SHRIMP & BEAN SALAD

IN ADDITION TO being a healthful first course, this dish makes a lovely lunch served with a loaf of crusty bread and a dry white wine. You may vary the proportions of beans to shrimp, depending on the occasion or the price of shrimp. The beans may be prepared a day in advance and kept in their cooking liquid in the refrigerator. Use a fruity, highly flavorful olive oil for this salad.

SERVES SIX

1 1/2 cups dried flageolets or black beans

The shrimp
1 cup dry white wine
1 quart water
1 carrot, sliced
2 stalks celery with tops, cut in large pieces
1 leek, well washed and cut in large pieces
1 tablespoon whole black peppercorns
2 bay leaves
1 1/2 to 2 pounds medium or large shrimp, peeled, deveined and washed

The bean salad
5 tablespoons extra virgin olive oil
3 cloves garlic, chopped
1 bunch green onions, chopped
1/4 cup flat-leaf parsley, chopped
1/4 cup fresh cilantro, chopped
1/4 cup fresh basil leaves, chopped
1/4 cup fresh lime juice
1 teaspoon salt
1/2 teaspoon freshly ground pepper
6 handfuls mixed salad greens, washed and dried

To Prepare the Beans: Soak or cook the dried beans as directed on page 165. Leave the beans in the cooking liquid and set aside.

To Prepare the Shrimp: Place the white wine, water, carrots, celery, leeks, peppercorns, and bay leaves in a large pot and bring to a boil. Reduce heat and simmer for 20 minutes. Strain, discard the vegetables, return the liquid to the pot, and bring to a boil. Add the shrimp, stir, remove the pot from the heat, and allow the shrimp to sit for about 5 to 7 minutes. (Cooking time varies with the size of the shrimp. To avoid overcooking, test them by cutting one shrimp in half after about 4 minutes.

†WINE SUGGESTION

Daniel Emerman, proprietor of Barocco, recommends a young Arneis des Roeri, produced by Giovanni Almondo, to accompany the Warm Shrimp & Bean Salad. To serve with the Roast Rack of Lamb he suggests a Rosso di Montalcino, 1990 produced by Mastrojanni.

The cooked shrimp should be firm, opaque, and pale pink throughout.) Drain the shrimp and place them in a large warm ceramic bowl. Set aside while you prepare the bean salad. Work quickly so the shrimp stay warm.

To Prepare the Bean Salad: Remove the beans from the liquid with a slotted spoon and place them in a medium-sized bowl. Add 1/2 cup of liquid from the beans, as well as the olive oil, garlic, green onions, parsley, cilantro, basil, lime juice, salt, and pepper. Mix well and check for seasoning.

To Serve: Arrange the salad greens on individual plates, top with the bean salad, and arrange the warm shrimp decoratively on top of each portion. Serve immediately.

BAROCCO ROAST RACK
OF LAMB

THIS PREPARATION OF rack of lamb is exquisite. It is simple to prepare, and chopping the garlic and rosemary together by hand offers one of the great pleasures of cooking as the emerging fragrances fill the air. The 24 hours of marinating not only adds flavor to the lamb but tenderizes the meat so that it just melts in your mouth. When you buy the lamb ask your butcher to "French" the racks, to trim away all but a thin layer of fat, and to shorten the chop bones to 3 or 4 inches.

SERVES SIX

2 racks of lamb (usually 7 or 8 rib chops per rack)
1 whole head garlic, peeled
1 bunch fresh rosemary (about 1 cup loosely
    packed sprigs)
2 tablespoons coarse salt
1 tablespoon coarsely ground black pepper
1 cup extra virgin olive oil

Dry the racks of lamb thoroughly. Chop the garlic and rosemary together and combine in a small bowl with the salt and pepper. Mix together well. Drizzle the racks with half of the olive oil and rub the seasoning mixture into the meat. Massage the meat well with the oil and the seasoning mixture. Cover with plastic wrap and refrigerate for 24 to 48 hours.

Remove the lamb from the refrigerator an hour before you plan to cook it. Place it in a shallow roasting pan with the rib bones pointing downward.

Preheat the oven to 500 degrees. Drizzle the
remaining olive oil over the meat. Roast the lamb
for 10 minutes to sear it. Then reduce the heat to
400 degrees and cook the lamb another 5 to 10
minutes until done to your taste. Chef Prosperi
recommends serving it rare to medium rare (130
degrees on a meat thermometer). Be careful not to
overcook it.

Remove the meat from the pan, cover it with a
towel, and let it rest for 10 to 15 minutes. Carve
the racks and serve 2 chops per person.

BAROCCO ROASTED POTATOES WITH FRESH SAGE & ROSEMARY

THIS WONDERFUL SIDE dish of roasted potatoes may well become a staple in your repertoire
because it goes just as well with roasted chicken as
it does with lamb or other meats. You can prepare
the potatoes ahead of time and reheat them while
the lamb is resting.

SERVES SIX

4 to 6 large Idaho potatoes, or 10 to 12 red
   potatoes, peeled and cut into 3/4-inch cubes
1 cup extra virgin olive oil
1 whole head garlic, separated into cloves but left
   unpeeled
3 sprigs fresh rosemary, leaves only
1 bunch fresh sage leaves (3/4 cup loosely
   packed)
salt
freshly ground pepper

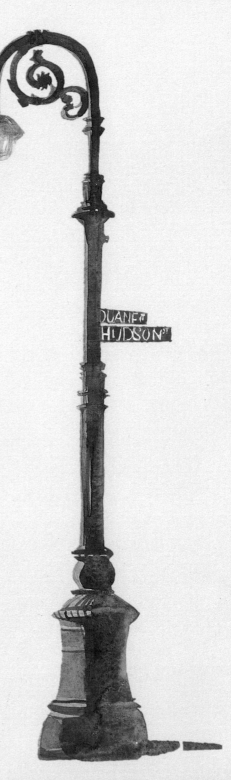

Soak the potato cubes in a bowl of ice water until you are ready to cook them. Preheat oven to 400 degrees.

Heat the olive oil in a heavy skillet over high heat. Thoroughly dry the potatoes and place them in the hot oil. Cook the potatoes, searing them on all sides, and tossing them to keep them from sticking. When the potatoes are lightly colored, add the garlic, stir well, and cook for 2 more minutes.

Remove from the heat and put the potatoes, oil, and garlic into a baking pan that can accommodate all of the potatoes in one layer. Scatter the rosemary and sage leaves on top of the potatoes. Season liberally with salt and freshly ground pepper. Roast for about 40 minutes, stirring occasionally until golden brown. Remove the potatoes with a slotted spoon and serve immediately.

BAROCCO HAZELNUT & ALMOND CAKE WITH MACERATED BERRIES & WHIPPED CREAM

THIS CAKE KEEPS very well and is delicious even without the fruit. It can be made a day ahead and stored in an airtight container until ready to serve. This recipe will generously serve six, allowing for leftovers. Consider this recipe when planning a buffet for a large crowd or when bringing dessert to a party, because it travels well.

Grind the hazelnuts and almonds in a food processor using the pulse button. The nuts should be finely and evenly ground. Be careful not to overprocess them or they will turn into nut butter.

For this cake, Chef Prosperi recommends using strawberries, loganberries, and blackberries. You can also use raspberries if you leave them whole; raspberries are too soft to be macerated.

MAKES ONE 9-INCH ROUND CAKE

The cake
7 ounces hazelnuts
5 ounces blanched almonds
1 tablespoon ground espresso
1/2 teaspoon baking powder
8 eggs, separated
zest of 1 orange
2/3 cup sugar
3 tablespoons butter, melted and cooled to room temperature
2 tablespoons hazelnut liqueur

The berries and whipped cream
4 cups of seasonal berries, washed and hulled
juice of 1 orange
juice of 1/2 lemon
1/4 cup Grand Marnier
2 tablespoons sugar
1/2 pint heavy cream

To Make the Cake: Preheat oven to 350 degrees. Butter and flour a deep 9-inch round cake pan or springform pan. Line the bottom with waxed paper or parchment paper. Then butter and flour the paper lining.

Finely grind the nuts in the bowl of a food processor. (You should get 1 3/4 cups of ground hazelnuts and 1 1/4 cups of ground almonds.) Place the ground nuts in a bowl and mix in the espresso. Transfer this mixture to a large cookie sheet or jelly-roll pan and distribute evenly. Toast in the oven until lightly browned, about 10 minutes. (Halfway through the cooking time, stir and redistribute the mixture evenly in the pan to make sure it is not browning too quickly on the bottom.) Remove from the oven and stir in the baking powder. (Keep the oven on.)

Beat together the egg yolks, zest of orange, and sugar in a large bowl until the mixture is pale yellow and forms a ribbon.

In another large bowl, beat the egg whites until soft peaks form. Fold one third of the egg-yolk mixture into the beaten egg whites, followed by one third of the nut mixture, followed by one third of the melted butter. Repeat this procedure until all of the cake ingredients are combined. Pour the batter into the prepared pan and bake for 45 minutes, or until a toothpick inserted in the center comes out clean.

Allow the cake to cool slightly. Then brush the top with half of the hazelnut liqueur. Turn the cake out to cool on a wire rack. Remove the paper from the bottom of the cake and brush with the remaining hazelnut liqueur.

To Prepare Berries: About an hour before serving, combine the berries, orange juice, lemon juice, Grand Marnier, and sugar in a glass or ceramic bowl. Mash the berries with the back of a fork or a pastry blender. Just before serving, whip the cream until it forms soft peaks.

To Serve: Arrange berries over each slice of cake. Add a tablespoon of the macerating liquid and a dollop of whipped cream on top.

CAPSOUTO FRÈRES

Spring Menu

SMOKED SALMON
RILLETTES

GRILLED
PORTOBELLO
MUSHROOMS
WITH BALSAMIC
VINAIGRETTE

HAZELNUT-
CRUSTED FILLET
OF RED SNAPPER
WITH CARDAMOM
BERCY SAUCE

STRAWBERRY
GINGER RHUBARB
CRISP

SMOKED SALMON RILLETTES

THIS RICH APPETIZER is perfect to serve with cocktails. The dish can be made up to four days in advance and refrigerated. Remove the rillettes from the refrigerator about half an hour before serving, to soften and enhance the flavors. Consider this recipe when planning a party; it can easily be increased to serve a crowd. In that case, you may want to spread the rillettes mixture onto the toasted baguettes and arrange them on a serving dish.

SERVES SIX

1/4 pound smoked salmon, sliced
1 dash cayenne pepper
1 dash nutmeg
2 teaspoons fresh tarragon, chopped
1 egg yolk
2 tablespoons olive oil
8 tablespoons butter, softened to room temperature
1 tablespoon lemon juice
1 baguette

To Make the Rillettes: Blend the salmon with the cayenne, nutmeg, and tarragon in the bowl of a food processor. Add the egg yolk while the processor is on. When the egg yolk is fully blended, add the olive oil in a steady stream. Then stop the machine and scrape down the sides of the bowl. Add the butter and continue to process, using the pulse button. Add the lemon juice and pulse until all of the ingredients are well incorporated. Adjust the seasoning. Transfer the finished mixture to a serving dish. Cover and chill.

To Serve: Thinly slice the baguette into rounds and toast them lightly. Arrange the rounds on a platter and serve with the rillettes.

†WINE SUGGESTION

Jacques Capsouto recommends the following types of French wine to be served with this menu: to accompany the Salmon Rillettes, a Pouilly-Fumé from the Loire Valley; with the Grilled Portobello Mushrooms, a Tokay from Alsace; a Chassagne Montrachet from Burgundy with the Hazelnut-Crusted Fillet of Red Snapper; and with the Strawberry Ginger Rhubarb Crisp, a Muscat de Beaumes de Venise from the southern Rhône.

CAPSOUTO FRÈRES · GRILLED PORTOBELLO MUSHROOMS WITH BALSAMIC VINAIGRETTE

PORTOBELLO MUSHROOMS HAVE a full, fresh flavor. They are now readily available year-round in grocery stores, but you will find the highest quality portobellos and the best prices at farmer's markets in the late spring through the fall. This recipe uses only the caps of the mushrooms. Reserve the stems for the Cardamom Bercy Sauce used in the next recipe.

SERVES SIX

The vinaigrette
1/2 cup extra virgin olive oil
1 shallot, finely chopped
1 clove garlic, finely chopped
1/2 cup light salad oil
1/2 cup balsamic vinegar
salt and freshly ground pepper

The mushrooms
6 large portobello mushroom
    caps
salt and freshly ground pepper
6 large handfuls seasonal salad greens,
    washed and dried

To Prepare the Balsamic Vinaigrette: Heat 1 tablespoon of the olive oil in a small sauté pan at a low temperature. Add the shallots and garlic and cook slowly until they are soft and turn pale yellow. Remove the shallots and garlic from the pan immediately and transfer them to a large glass or ceramic bowl. Set aside to cool. Add the remaining olive oil as well as the salad oil and vinegar. Season with salt and pepper to taste. Set aside.

To Prepare the Mushrooms: Start the grill and let it heat up while you prepare the mushrooms. Gently wash the mushroom caps in warm water, brushing away any dirt. Pat them dry and season them with salt and pepper.

When the grill is ready, dip each mushroom cap in the vinaigrette, coating both sides, and place topside down on the grill. Cook the mushrooms for 4 to 6 minutes. (Halfway through the grilling time, lift the mushrooms from the grill and rotate each one a quarter turn to give an attractive cross hatch grill mark.) Turn the mushrooms over and cook 4 to 6 minutes on the other side. (Again, halfway through grilling, rotate the mushrooms a quarter turn to give them a cross hatch mark on the other side.)

To Serve: Place the salad greens on 6 individual plates. Arrange the grilled mushrooms on top of the greens, and drizzle with additional balsamic vinaigrette.

CAPSOUTO FRÈRES

HAZELNUT-CRUSTED FILLET OF RED SNAPPER WITH CARDAMOM BERCY SAUCE

THIS DISH USES classic French techniques and adds an exotic twist with the dusky flavor of cardamom, which marries well with the hazelnuts and the red snapper. The sauce may be prepared earlier in the day and reheated before serving. The recipe calls for mushroom stems, although they are optional. Use the stems from the mushrooms in the previous recipe, Grilled Portobello Mushrooms with Balsamic Vinaigrette. We recommend serving the fish with rice or orzo.

SERVES SIX

The sauce

2 tablespoons olive oil
1 large onion, finely chopped
5 shallots, finely chopped
5 cloves garlic, finely chopped
2 red snappers, bones, tails, skins, trimmings, and heads only
2 tablespoons ground cardamom
pinch of freshly ground pepper
1 cup mushroom stems, chopped (optional)
2 cups dry white wine
1 quart veal stock
salt
freshly ground pepper

The red snapper

1 cup hazelnuts, toasted
4 tablespoons ground cardamom
1/2 cup flour
2 eggs
1/2 cup heavy cream
salt
freshly ground pepper
6 small fillets of red snapper, skinned
1 cup Wondra flour for dredging
2 tablespoons light soy oil
3 to 6 tablespoons butter
1/2 cup chopped fresh parsley for garnish

To Prepare the Sauce: Heat the olive oil in a large pot over a medium-high temperature. Sauté the onion, shallots, and garlic in the olive oil until brown. Add the fish and cook for about 15 minutes, or until the bones are broken up. Stir in the cardamom, pinch of pepper, and optional mushroom stems. Then add the wine and reduce the liquid almost completely. Add the veal stock and continue cooking for about 45 minutes, reducing the liquid by half, until it resembles a thin syrup. Remove from the heat and strain the liquid. Discard the residual solids. If the sauce is too thin, reduce it further. Season with salt and pepper to taste.

To Prepare the Fish: Place the hazelnuts in the bowl of a food processor. Break them up by processing, using the pulse button. Add the cardamom and flour and continue processing using the pulse button, until the nuts are finely ground. Transfer the mixture to a large plate or cookie sheet and set it aside.

In a medium-sized bowl, beat the eggs and cream together and season the mixture with salt and pepper.

Pat the fillets dry with a paper towel. Season them with salt and pepper. Dredge each fillet in Wondra flour and shake off the excess flour. Dip the fillet in egg mixture and shake off the excess egg. Finally, coat both sides of the fish evenly with the nut mixture.

Heat the soy oil in a large sauté pan over medium-high heat. Place the fillets in the pan, along with a small piece of butter. Sauté the fish for 2 to 3 minutes. Turn the fish over and cook the other side 2 to 3 minutes, or until the flesh firms up. (You may need to cook the fillets in batches. If so, add oil and butter to the pan as needed.) Transfer the fillets to a platter and keep them warm. Meanwhile, warm the dinner plates.

To Serve: On each of 6 warm dinner plates, place one fish fillet. Spoon the Cardamom Bercy Sauce over the fish, and sprinkle chopped parsley on top. Place a portion of rice or orzo alongside the fish and serve immediately.

CAPSOUTO FRÈRES STRAWBERRY GINGER RHUBARB CRISP

THE GINGER RHUBARB jam gives this crisp a very special flavor that distinguishes it from other fruit crisps. At Capsouto Frères, Chef Tutino makes up large quantities of this jam so he can continue to serve the crisp long after rhubarb is no longer in season. The ginger rhubarb jam recipe will make enough for two crisps. Chef Tutino does not recommend cutting this recipe in half. Instead, make the full recipe and freeze some to enjoy with the fall crop of strawberries.

SERVES SIX

The ginger rhubarb jam
1 pound fresh rhubarb, washed and trimmed and
  cut into 1-inch pieces

1 tablespoon fresh ginger, finely diced
2 tablespoons lemon juice
2/3 cup sugar
1/2 cup water

The filling
2 pint baskets of strawberries, washed
    and hulled
1 cup ginger rhubarb jam
1/3 cup light brown sugar, packed
juice of 1 lemon

The crisp
1 cup flour
1 cup sugar
3/4 teaspoon salt
1 teaspoon baking powder
1/2 teaspoon cinnamon
1/2 teaspoon mace
1 egg
1/3 cup melted butter

To Make the Jam: Combine the rhubarb, ginger and lemon juice in a large nonre-active bowl. Set aside.

Combine the sugar and water in a large saucepan and bring the liquid to a boil. Continue cooking, stirring occa-sionally, until the syrup reaches the soft-ball stage—that is, when it forms a soft ball when dropped into a cup of cold water (236 degrees on a candy thermometer).

Add the rhubarb mixture and stir well. Return the mixture to a boil and cook for another 3 to 5 minutes, or until the fruit is soft.

Remove the pan from the heat and allow the jam to cool to room temperature. Reserve one cup for the crisp and store the remainder in a container, covered tightly.

To Make the Filling: If the berries are small, leave them whole. If they are large, cut them in half. Combine the strawberries with the jam, brown sugar, and lemon juice in a large nonreactive bowl. Set aside for up to one hour.

To Make the Crisp: Preheat the oven to 375 degrees. Butter a 10-inch round pie plate or other low-sided baking dish. Combine the flour, sugar, salt, baking powder, cinnamon, and mace in a large bowl. Lightly beat the egg and stir it into the dry ingredients with a fork until the mixture is crumbly.

Fill the pie plate with the fruit mixture and sprinkle the crumb mixture evenly on top. Pour the melted butter evenly over the crumb mixture. Bake for 25 to 30 minutes until lightly browned and bubbling. (Place a baking sheet or piece of aluminum foil beneath the crisp to catch drips.) Cool the fruit crisp on a wire rack for at least 5 minutes.

To Serve: Serve at room temperature or warm from the oven with vanilla ice cream.

THE CLEAVER COMPANY

A Spring Buffet

ASPARAGUS,
MORELS, RAMPS
& FIDDLEHEAD
FERNS WITH
ORANGE OIL &
EDIBLE FLOWERS

PASTA WITH
SAUTÉED GREENS
& ROASTED
GARLIC

GRILLED
CHICKEN SALAD
WITH THAI
DRESSING

OLIVE
BREADSTICKS

SAVORY CORN
MADELEINES

STRAWBERRY
BREAD PUDDING

ASPARAGUS, MORELS, RAMPS & FIDDLEHEAD FERNS WITH ORANGE OIL & EDIBLE FLOWERS

THIS DISH TRULY speaks of the season. Ramps are baby wild leeks that have a heavy pungent flavor similar to that of garlic chives. Ramps and fiddlehead ferns are available for only a brief time in the spring. Morels are one of the first mushrooms of spring. If these ingredients are unavailable, don't hesitate to make the asparagus alone with the orange oil. You can make the orange oil up to two weeks in advance and store it in the refrigerator in an airtight container. Whisk the liquid before serving.

SERVES EIGHT

The orange oil
2 cups fresh orange juice
1/4 cup olive oil

The vegetables
1/2 pound fiddlehead ferns
1 bunch ramps, about 4 inches in diameter
4 tablespoons olive oil
1/2 pound fresh morels, lightly brushed or quickly washed if necessary
1 tablespoon butter
2 1/2 pounds asparagus, trimmed and cleaned
1/4 cup water
pinch of salt
several edible flowers such as nasturtiums, pansies, or marigolds, for garnish

To Make the Orange Oil: Heat the orange juice in a nonreactive saucepan. Cook over high heat for about 30 minutes until the liquid reduces to 1/4 cup of thick syrup. (The syrup should darken only slightly toward the end of the reduction. Watch carefully to avoid burning.) Remove the pan from the heat and transfer the syrup to a bowl. Add the olive oil in a steady stream, whisking to thoroughly incorporate. Set aside.

†WINE SUGGESTION

The Cleaver Company relies on inspired wine advice from New York's Rosenthal Wine Merchants when planning special events. Rosenthal's recommends a Casis Blanc, Domaine du Bagnol and a Bandol Rosé, Château Pradeaux, to be served throughout the spring buffet menu.

To Prepare the Vegetables: Rub the fiddlehead ferns to remove as much of the chaff as possible. Drop them in a large pot of boiling water and leave them for 2 to 3 minutes, until the greens are blanched. Drain the fiddlehead ferns and set them aside.

Clean the ramps as you would green onions. Then finely chop the white bulbs and part of the green stem. Reserve the leafy tops. Heat 2 tablespoons of the olive oil in a medium-sized sauté pan and sauté the ramps for about 2 minutes until they begin to soften. Add the morels and continue to sauté for about 4 minutes, until they are tender. Remove the pan from the heat and set aside.

In a large sauté pan over medium heat, melt the butter and stir in the remaining 2 tablespoons of olive oil. Add the asparagus, water, and salt. Sauté for 4 to 5 minutes, tossing the asparagus frequently. (You may need to do this in batches, depending on the size of your pan.)

To Serve: Line the bottom of a serving platter with the reserved leafy tops of the ramps. Fan the asparagus over this leafy lining. Scatter the sautéed ramps and morels over the asparagus, trying not to cover the tips of the asparagus. Then place the fiddlehead ferns on top. Pour the orange oil in a zig-zag pattern over the asparagus. Garnish the platter with the edible flowers. Serve at room temperature.

THE CLEAVER COMPANY

PASTA WITH SAUTÉED GREENS & ROASTED GARLIC

THIS DELICIOUS SIDE dish can be made with any combination of young spring greens. If you use red chard, it will tint the pasta, which makes for a colorful presentation. The first step in this recipe is to roast the garlic. This can be done several hours in advance.

SERVES EIGHT

2 heads garlic, left whole and unpeeled
4 tablespoons olive oil
1 pound dried pasta (such as penne, fusilli, or bowties)
1 1/2 pounds spring greens (such as red chard, green chard, mustard greens, spinach, dandelion greens, or sorrel) washed, trimmed, and coarsely chopped
3 tablespoons fresh lemon juice
salt
freshly ground pepper

To Roast the Garlic: Preheat the oven to 350 degrees. Place the heads of garlic on a piece of aluminum foil. Drizzle 1 tablespoon of olive oil over them and wrap them in the foil. Bake the garlic for 45 minutes to 1 hour until it is soft. Remove the garlic from the oven, unwrap it, and let it cool. Squeeze the pulp from the hulls and reserve.

To Make the Pasta and Greens: Bring salted water to a boil in a large pot and cook the pasta until it is al dente. Drain and toss the cooked pasta with 1 tablespoon of olive oil.

While the pasta is cooking, heat the remaining 2 tablespoons of olive oil in a large sauté pan and add the greens. Cook them for a few minutes, tossing frequently, until they are wilted. (Add a little water to the greens if necessary.)

To Serve: Transfer the pasta and greens to a serving bowl. Add the lemon juice and garlic, and season with salt and pepper to taste. Toss well and adjust the seasoning. Serve this dish at room temperature.

THE CLEAVER COMPANY

GRILLED CHICKEN SALAD WITH THAI DRESSING

MUCH OF THE simple preparation for this dish can be done ahead of time. You can either sauté the chicken on the stove or grill it over charcoal. Dress and serve the chicken warm or at room temperature.

SERVES EIGHT

The marinade and chicken
1/4 cup garlic, peeled and chopped (about
    1/2 a large head)
1/4 cup fresh lime juice (about 2 to 3 limes)
1/4 cup white wine
1/2 cup olive oil
2 tablespoons fresh thyme, chopped
2 tablespoons fresh rosemary, chopped
pinch of freshly ground pepper
5 whole chicken breasts—boned, skinned,
    and split

The dressing
3 tablespoons Thai fish sauce
1/4 cup fresh lime juice
3/4 cup olive oil
1/2 cup green onions (1 bunch), cleaned and
    finely chopped
2 large carrots, peeled and cut into 2-inch juli-
    enned pieces
1/2 cup fresh mint, chopped
1/2 cup unsalted peanuts

2 heads spring field lettuce, washed and dried

To Marinate the Chicken: Mix together the garlic, lime juice, wine, olive oil, thyme, rosemary, and pepper in a medium-sized nonreactive bowl. Place the chicken in a large shallow dish and pour the marinade on top. Toss the chicken to coat it well with the marinade. Cover and refrigerate it for several hours or up to three days.

To Make the Dressing: Combine the fish sauce with the lime juice and olive oil. Whisk the liquids to blend them. Add the green onions, carrots, and mint. Stir in the peanuts. Set aside the dressing.

To Grill the Chicken: Prepare the grill, or heat a heavy sauté pan over high heat. Shake the excess marinade from the chicken. Then grill the chicken for about 7 minutes, turning it halfway through the cooking time to grill on both sides. (Or sear the chicken in the sauté pan, browning on both sides, and then continue to cook it over medium heat for about 7 minutes.) Remove from the heat and set the chicken aside.

To Serve: Arrange the lettuce on a serving platter. Slice each piece of chicken lengthwise and at a slight angle into 3 or 4 strips. Arrange the strips together on the greens. Pour the dressing over the chicken and the greens.

THE CLEAVER COMPANY

OLIVE BREADSTICKS

THESE BREADSTICKS, MADE from basic pizza dough, are very popular at the Cleaver Company store. They make a good addition to just about any lunch or dinner menu. This recipe describes a long breadstick, but you can make them any length you wish. You can freeze the dough for up to one month. After it rises, punch it down and freeze in an oiled sealable plastic bag, or freeze the shaped breadsticks. Be sure to thaw thoroughly before baking.

MAKES 12 BREADSTICKS

2 cups tepid water

1 package dry yeast (or 0.6 ounces fresh yeast)

2 tablespoons olive oil

1 1/2 cups semolina flour

2 teaspoons kosher salt

3 1/2 to 4 cups white flour

3/4 cup black Niçoise olives, pitted and finely chopped

THE **CLEAVER** COMPANY

CATERERS
229 WEST BROADWAY
NEW YORK, NY 10013

MARY CLEAVER
(212) 431-3688

Pour the water in the bowl of a 5-quart mixer fitted with a dough hook. Stir in the yeast to dissolve and allow it to sit for 2 minutes. Add 1 tablespoon of olive oil and mix well. Add the semolina flour and blend thoroughly. Add the kosher salt, then 3 1/2 cups of flour, 1 cup at a time, and beat until well mixed. The dough should pull away from the sides of the bowl and not be sticky. If necessary, add another 1/2 cup of flour. Beat the dough for 10 minutes or knead it by hand until it is elastic. Oil a large bowl with the remaining olive oil. Place the dough in the bowl and turn it over to coat the surface of the dough with oil. Cover the bowl with a towel or plastic wrap and keep in a warm place until the dough doubles in size.

Preheat the oven to 350 degrees. Lightly oil 2 large baking sheets, or line them with parchment paper. Stretch the dough into a rectangle about 12 x 5 inches. Distribute the olives evenly over the dough and roll it into a long cylinder. Cut it into 12 pieces and roll each piece into a thin cylinder, about 15 inches long.

Arrange the breadsticks on the baking sheets, spaced about 1 inch apart. Bake for about 15 minutes, or until they are light brown and easy to pick up. Cool on a wire rack. The breadsticks are best eaten within several hours of baking.

SAVORY CORN MADELEINES

THIS RECIPE PUTS a savory twist on the classic tea cake. These madeleines are simple to make and should be made as close to serving as possible. You may substitute just about any fresh herb for the sage.

MAKES 12 MADELEINES

5 tablespoons flour
1/4 cup cornmeal
3 tablespoons corn flour
1 tablespoon sugar
1 1/4 teaspoons baking powder
pinch of salt
1 egg

1 1/2 tablespoons melted butter
5 tablespoons buttermilk
1/2 tablespoon sage, finely chopped

Preheat the oven to 350 degrees. Generously butter and chill the madeleine pans. Combine the flour, cornmeal, corn flour, sugar, baking powder, and salt, and set this mixture aside. In a large mixing bowl, mix the egg, butter, and buttermilk together with a whisk. Add the sage and whisk together. Then fold in the flour mixture.

Distribute the batter equally among the prepared madeleine pans. Bake the madeleines about 15 minutes until they are golden brown and shrink a bit from the sides of the pans. Lift each one carefully from the pan, using a knife to loosen it. Cool the madeleines right-side up on a wire rack.

THE CLEAVER COMPANY	## STRAWBERRY BREAD PUDDING

BREAD PUDDING IS a very satisfying dessert. This one is especially good. Substitute any berries for the strawberries, depending on the season and what looks fresh at the market. If you don't have a baguette, use about six slices of stale white bread. Cut the crusts off first; then cut the slices into small cubes. This dessert can be made ahead of time and refrigerated. You can serve it cold or at room temperature, but it tastes best right from the oven.

SERVES EIGHT

I quart heavy cream
I vanilla bean, or I teaspoon vanilla extract
4 egg yolks
4 whole eggs
I cup sugar
I pint strawberries, hulled and sliced
I small baguette cut in cubes (about 4 cups loosely packed)

Preheat the oven to 325 degrees. Pour the cream in a heavy saucepan. Split the vanilla bean and scrape the seeds into the cream. Then drop the rest of the bean in the cream. Heat the cream at a medium-high temperature, just until it simmers. Remove the pan from the heat and allow the cream to cool until it almost reaches room temperature. Take the vanilla bean out and set the cream aside. Rinse the vanilla bean and set it aside to dry.*

Whisk the egg yolks and the whole eggs together in a nonreactive bowl. Add the sugar, whisking to combine. (If you did not use a vanilla bean, add the vanilla extract at this stage, and whisk to blend.) Add the cream to the egg mixture, whisking until the liquids combine. Stir in the sliced strawberries and bread.

Butter a 9 x 12 inch nonreactive baking dish. Spread the mixture in the dish. Place the dish in a larger pan. Pour hot water in the larger pan to about 1/2-inch deep. Bake the pudding for about 50 minutes, or until it is golden brown and a knife inserted into the center comes out clean.

Once the vanilla bean dries, you can place it in a container of sugar. The vanilla will gradually perfume the sugar. You can use this vanilla sugar in any recipes that call for vanilla and sugar.

NOSMO KING

Spring Menu

❦

ASPARAGUS WITH
HORSERADISH
VINAIGRETTE &
PICKLED BEETS

PAN-FRIED SOFT-
SHELL CRABS
WITH TOMATO
VINAIGRETTE &
FAVA BEANS
WITH SHALLOTS
& SUMMER
SAVORY

NAPOLEON OF
STRAWBERRIES &
SWEET YOGURT

ASPARAGUS WITH HORSERADISH VINAIGRETTE & PICKLED BEETS

THIS DISH COMBINES crisp colors and flavors enhanced by the use of fresh horseradish. If this ingredient is not available, use one quarter cup of prepared horseradish instead, but add only a little of the cider vinegar. This entire dish may be prepared in advance and assembled just before serving.

SERVES SIX

The beets
1 1/2 cups fresh beets, peeled and diced into 1/4 inch cubes
1 large piece fresh orange rind
1 cup red wine vinegar

The asparagus
30 large asparagus spears, peeled and trimmed.

The vinaigrette
1 small piece fresh horseradish, peeled and roughly chopped into 1-inch cubes (1/2 cup)
2 tablespoons lemon juice
6 tablespoons olive oil
2 tablespoons cider vinegar
salt
freshly ground pepper
parsley sprigs, for garnish

To Prepare the Beets: Place the beets in a medium-sized pot of lightly salted water. Add the orange rind. Bring the water to a boil over medium-high heat. Cook the beets until they are tender. Drain the beets and remove orange rind. Transfer the beets to a glass jar, cover them with the red wine vinegar, and let them cool. This step may be done up to one month in advance. Cover the jar and keep it in the refrigerator.

To Prepare the Asparagus: Steam the asparagus or boil it in salted water in a nonreactive saucepan over medium heat for about 5 minutes, or until a sharp knife inserts easily in the stem ends. Remove the asparagus from the saucepan and place it in ice water immediately. When the asparagus is cool, drain it, wrap it in a clean towel, and refrigerate it. This step may be done one day in advance.

✝ WINE SUGGESTION

Chef Alan Harding recommends Harpoon Stout or Catamount Amber beer to accompany the appetizer followed by a Sakonnet 1990 Pinot Noir from Rhode Island to accompany the main course.

To Make the Vinaigrette: Place the horseradish in a blender. Add the lemon juice and then add the olive oil slowly in a stream while the blender is running. Then add the cider vinegar. Season with salt and pepper to taste. The vinaigrette may be prepared in advance and will keep for one month in a tightly covered jar in the refrigerator.

To Serve: Place 5 spears of asparagus on each plate. Dress the asparagus with a generous tablespoon of vinaigrette. Garnish with the drained pickled beets and a sprig of parsley.

NOSMO KING PAN-FRIED SOFT-SHELL CRABS WITH TOMATO VINAIGRETTE & FAVA BEANS WITH SHALLOTS & SUMMER SAVORY

THIS CRAB DISH uses traditional seasonings and is enhanced by the flavors of the fresh tomato vinaigrette. The recipe for the fava beans with shallots and summer savory complements the crab very well. This meal is a good example of how Chef Harding exalts the classic American cuisine.

SERVES SIX

The vinaigrette
2 cups fresh tomatoes—peeled, seeded, and
    coarsely chopped
1/2 cup red wine vinegar
3/4 cup olive oil
salt

The beans
2 cups fresh fava beans, shelled (about
    2 pounds unshelled)
2 teaspoons olive oil
1/4 cup shallots, peeled and sliced
1 cup fresh tomatoes—peeled, seeded,
    and finely chopped
1 cup fish or vegetable stock
    (or water)

1 tablespoon fresh summer savory or
    fresh marjoram, chopped
salt
freshly ground pepper

The crabs
canola oil for frying
1 cup cornmeal
salt
freshly ground pepper
2 tablespoons Old Bay Seasoning
12 large soft-shell crabs, eyes and gills
    removed, and rinsed clean

To Make the Vinaigrette: Place the tomatoes in a blender or a food processor. Add the vinegar and blend. Slowly add the olive oil while the blender or food processor is running. Season with salt. Strain the vinaigrette and set it aside.

To Prepare the Beans: Blanch the fava beans in a large pot of boiling, salted water. Drain and rinse the beans immediately in cold water and peel them when cool to the touch. Heat the olive oil in a large sauté pan at a medium temperature. Add the shallots, tossing them until they are golden brown. Then add the fava beans, tomatoes, and stock. Increase the heat and continue cooking for about 5 minutes, or until the fava beans are tender. Stir in the summer savory, and add salt and pepper to taste.

To Cook the Crabs: Fill a large skillet with oil to a depth of 1/2 inch. Heat the oil until it begins to smoke. Meanwhile, stir together the cornmeal and Old Bay Seasoning in a small bowl. Season the crabs with salt and pepper, first lifting the shell flaps up. Dredge the crabs in the cornmeal mixture until they are thoroughly coated. Shake off the excess mixture. Fry the crabs over medium-high heat for 6 to 8 minutes, or until they are golden brown. (Halfway through the cooking time, turn them once. Soft-shell crabs pop and splatter while cooking, so be careful not to stand too close to the stove.) Transfer the crabs to a warm platter, and keep them warm.

To Serve: Place two crabs in the center of each of 6 warm dinner plates. Serve the fava beans and tomato vinaigrette on opposite sides of the crabs.

<table>
</table>

NOSMO KING

NAPOLEON OF STRAWBERRIES & SWEET YOGURT

USUALLY NAPOLEONS AREN'T considered to be lean desserts. Prepared as they are at Nosmo King though, they are surprisingly low in fat. And they are every bit as delicious as the traditional version. You will be able to do most of the preparation for this dessert in advance. The final assembly can take place just before serving.

SERVES SIX

16 ounces sheeps' milk or goats' milk yogurt
5 tablespoons honey
pinch of nutmeg
4 tablespoons canola oil
4 teaspoons vanilla
8 sheets phyllo dough
2 pints strawberries, thinly sliced
additional honey for garnish
2 tablespoons macadamia nuts,
    toasted and crushed, for garnish
6 sprigs fresh mint for garnish

To Prepare the Yogurt Filling: One day in advance, line the inside of a strainer with a piece of cheesecloth. Rest the strainer over a deep bowl. Spoon the yogurt onto the cheesecloth and allow it to drain overnight, refrigerated. The next day, discard the whey and mix together the strained yogurt, honey, and nutmeg in a ceramic or glass bowl. Set aside.

To Prepare the Phyllo: Preheat the oven to 400 degrees. In a small bowl, mix the oil and vanilla together. Place one sheet of phyllo on a flat surface. Cover the remaining sheets with a damp dish towel to prevent them from drying out. Brush the phyllo sheet very lightly with a little of the oil mixture. Place another sheet of phyllo on top and repeat until you have used four sheets, moistening each one lightly with the oil mixture.

Lightly grease the bottoms of two baking sheets. Slip one baking sheet (upside-down) under the stack of prepared phyllo sheets. Place the other baking sheet on top. (This will keep the dough flat as it bakes.) Bake for 6 minutes, or until golden brown. Remove from the oven and place on a wire rack to cool. Meanwhile, prepare the remaining four sheets of phyllo in the same way, and bake them as you did the first batch.

Cut each stack of phyllo in thirds lengthwise. Cut each of these sections into thirds, too, so you have nine equal-sized rectangles. Repeat with the other stack of phyllo. Set these pieces aside in a cool, dry place until you are ready to assemble the Napoleons.

To Assemble: Each Napoleon will use three phyllo rectangles. Alternate layers of phyllo, yogurt, and strawberries, starting and ending with phyllo. Place each Napoleon on a dessert plate. Drizzle a thin stream of honey over each Napoleon. Garnish with crushed nuts and a sprig of mint.

TRIBECA GRILL

*A Four-Course Tasting Menu**

❧

SAUTÉE OF FOIE GRAS WITH PARSNIPS & SWEET AND SOUR CHERRIES

PAILLARD OF SALMON IN FRESH LAURIER VINAIGRETTE WITH LEEKS, TOMATOES & ASPARAGUS

SQUAB WITH YOUNG MORELS, ROAST GARLIC & SAGE POLENTA

WARM CASHEW *FINANCIER* WITH FROZEN MASCARPONE MOUSSE, COFFEE ANGLAISE, CHOCOLATE SAUCE & CANDIED CASHEWS

SAUTÉ OF FOIE GRAS WITH PARSNIPS & SWEET AND SOUR CHERRIES

THIS DISH HAS an interesting combination of textures and flavors. Timing is important with this dish. Place the parsnip purée and the parsnip chips on warm plates and have the cherry sauce ready before you cook the foie gras. In fact, the guests should be seated at the table while the foie gras is cooking. That way, you will be able to serve the dish at its best. If fresh cherries are not available, you can substitute canned tart cherries, packed in water, and frozen dark sweet cherries.

SERVES SIX

The parsnips
1 1/2 pounds parsnips, peeled and trimmed
2 tablespoons butter
1/2 cup water
vegetable oil for frying

The cherries
1/3 cup sugar
1/3 cup sherry vinegar
1 cup black cherries, split and pitted
1 cup red cherries, split and pitted

The foie gras
3/4 pound grade A foie gras, in 2-ounce portions

†WINE SUGGESTION

David Gordon, Wine Director for Tribeca Grill has selected the following wines to be enjoyed with this meal: with the Sauté of Foie Gras a Domaine-Zind Humbrecht Gewürztraminer Hengst, 1989; with the Paillard of Salmon a Rex Hill Pinot Gris, 1992; with the Squab with Young Morels a Château Beaucastel Châteauneuf-du-Pape, 1990; and with the Warm Cashew Financier a Taylor Fladgate and Yeatman 20-Year-Old Tawny port.

A tasting menu provides the diner with modest portions of several dishes. If you select one of the first three courses to serve as a main dish, you may wish to consider increasing the portions recommended here, or you may wish to serve an additional side dish of vegetables, pasta, or rice. You would not need to increase the dessert recipe, however, because it is already intended for individual portions.

To Prepare the Puréed Parsnips: With a mandoline or sharp knife, shave the parsnips to get twelve long slivers, about 1/16-inch thick. Set aside these slivers for the parsnip chips. Coarsely chop the remaining parsnips. Heat the butter and water in a heavy saucepan and steam the chopped parsnips, covered, over low heat until they soften and the water is absorbed. (Check them often, because parsnips cook quickly.) Remove from the heat. Purée the parsnips until smooth, using a food processor. Return the purée to the pan, cover it, and keep warm until ready to serve. Meanwhile, make the cherry sauce.

To Prepare the Sauce: In a heavy saucepan over medium heat, caramelize the sugar until it is a deep golden brown. Remove the pan from the heat and add the vinegar. Return it to the heat and cook for 5 minutes. Add the cherries and cook at a low temperature for about 5 minutes. Remove the pan from the heat and set aside.

To Fry the Parsnip Chips: Pour the oil in a large sauté pan, wok, or casserole to a depth of 1/2 inch. Heat the oil over medium-high heat until it is hot but not smoking. Fry the parsnip chips until they are crispy. Drain them on paper towels.

To Cook the Foie Gras and Serve: Heat a dry sauté pan over high heat. When the pan is very hot, brown the pieces of foie gras well on one side. Then turn them over and cook them for about 30 seconds. To serve, transfer the foie gras to the warm plates on which the parsnip purée and chips have been placed. Spoon the sauce on top.

TRIBECA GRILL — PAILLARD OF SALMON IN FRESH LAURIER VINAIGRETTE WITH LEEKS, TOMATOES & ASPARAGUS

PINK SALMON, COMBINED with fresh green asparagus and accented by red tomatoes and opaque leeks, makes a beautiful and delicious dish. Laurier Vinaigrette takes its name and its flavor from fresh bay leaves. The vinaigrette recipe yields enough to serve with as much as 2 1/4 pounds of salmon. This sauce can be made earlier in the day and reheated before serving. Also, you can blanch the vegetables beforehand, and the salmon takes just moments to cook. This all adds up to a dish that goes quickly from oven to table.

SERVES SIX

The salmon
1 1/2 pounds salmon fillet
salt
freshly ground pepper

The vegetables
3 small spring leeks, with tops trimmed off
1 tablespoon olive oil
1 pound medium-sized asparagus, trimmed
2 medium tomatoes

The vinaigrette
2 shallots, minced
2 cloves garlic, minced
6 tablespoons olive oil
1 1/2 cups dry white wine
2 fresh bay leaves
2 1/2 teaspoons tomato paste
2 tablespoons fresh lemon juice
2 tablespoons red wine vinegar
salt
freshly ground pepper
4 tablespoons butter, softened to room
    temperature

To Prepare the Salmon: Butter two baking sheets. Thinly slice the salmon, holding the knife at a diagonal and cutting in the same fashion as for smoked salmon. (The pieces will be irregular in size and shape.) Place the slices on the baking sheets in neatly overlapping pieces to form six circles, each about five inches in diameter. Refrigerate the salmon for at least one hour. Meanwhile, prepare the vegetables.

To Prepare the Vegetables: Quarter the leeks lengthwise and clean them thoroughly. Pat them dry. Heat the olive oil in a large saucepan over medium-low heat and add the leeks, stirring gently to coat them with the oil.

Cover the pan immediately and sweat the leeks (see page 166) until they are wilted but not browned. Remove the pan from the heat and set aside.

Drop the asparagus in a large pot of boiling water for 30 seconds to blanch. Lift the asparagus from the boiling water and place them in ice water for a few minutes. (Reserve the boiling water.)

Plunge the tomatoes into the boiling water for 30 seconds. Remove them immediately. Peel, seed, and dice the tomatoes. Set aside. Meanwhile, prepare the vinaigrette.

To Make the Vinaigrette: Place the shallots, garlic, and olive oil in a small saucepan over low heat for 10 minutes, stirring occasionally. Add the wine and bay leaves. Raise the heat and cook for 15 to 20 minutes, until the mixture reduces by about three-fourths. Add the tomato paste, lemon juice, vinegar, salt, and pepper. Bring the mixture to a boil and remove immediately from the heat. (If you are preparing the sauce ahead of time, stop at this point. Then resume when you are ready to serve the dish.) Remove the bay leaves and slowly whisk in the softened butter. Adjust the seasoning if necessary.

To Cook the Salmon and Serve: Preheat the broiler. Remove the salmon from the refrigerator and season it well with salt and pepper. Broil the salmon for about 3 minutes. (Be careful not to overcook it.) Carefully slide each circle of salmon slices from the baking sheet using a metal spatula. Transfer the circles to warm plates. Spoon the warm vinaigrette over the salmon. Garnish it with the leeks, asparagus, and tomatoes. Serve immediately.

TRIBECA GRILL

Squab with Young Morels, Roast Garlic & Sage Polenta

THIS RECIPE TAKES two days to complete. On the first day you will marinate the squab and make the garlic broth. Squab are surprisingly meaty birds. Marinating them overnight ensures that the meat will be tender and full of flavor. The roasted garlic broth is a robust flavor enhancer that can be used in sauces and for risotto. Although it is not essential, preparing the broth a day ahead will strengthen its flavor even more. It's best to cook the polenta just before serving it. The timing works well with cooking the squab.

SERVES SIX

The garlic broth

1 whole head garlic, separated into cloves but left unpeeled
1 tablespoon olive oil
3 cups strong chicken broth

The squab

4 large shallots, coarsely chopped

2 cloves garlic, coarsely chopped

2 tablespoons olive oil

1 cup Zinfandel

2 bay leaves

3 sprigs thyme

10 to 15 black peppercorns

6 young squab, breastbone removed

The polenta and morels

1 1/2 cups cornmeal

1 tablespoon butter

1/2 cup crème fraîche

10 leaves fresh sage, chopped

1 teaspoon salt

1 teaspoon freshly ground white pepper

2 cups fresh morels, or 1/4 cup dried morels
    (soaked to reconstitute and towel dried)

2 tablespoons olive oil

To Prepare the Garlic Broth: Preheat the oven to 300 degrees. Toss the garlic cloves with the olive oil and wrap them loosely in aluminum foil. Roast the garlic for 30 minutes. Remove from the oven and cool. Then peel the cloves. Pour the chicken broth into a large saucepan and add the garlic. Bring the broth to a boil and simmer gently, half-covered, for 30 minutes. Remove from the heat and set aside. Let the broth stand overnight, or until you are ready to make the polenta.

To Marinate and Cook the Squab: In a small sauté pan, lightly sauté the shallots and garlic in the olive oil over a medium heat until they are soft but not browned. Transfer the shallots and garlic to a one-pint measuring cup or jar and add the wine, bay leaves, thyme, and peppercorns.

Place the squab in a single layer along the bottom of a nonreactive baking dish. Pour the marinade over the squab. Cover and refrigerate overnight.

Preheat the oven to 375 degrees. Place the squab, breast-side up, in a large roasting pan. Discard the marinade. Roast the squab for 40 to 50 minutes, or until the juices of the breast meat run clear when you poke the squab with a fork. Meanwhile, make the polenta.

To Make the Polenta: Remove the garlic from the broth. If you wish, rub a few of the softened cloves of garlic through a fine mesh strainer into the broth, using the back of a wooden spoon. Bring the broth to a boil again. Add the cornmeal slowly to the broth in a steady stream, whisking constantly to combine until all of the

cornmeal is incorporated and the mixture thickens. Lower the heat as much as possible and cook the polenta for 20 minutes, stirring from time to time. Add the butter, crème fraîche, sage, salt, and pepper just before serving, stirring well to incorporate.

To Serve: Just before serving, sauté the morels briefly in olive oil over high heat. Place the squab on individual plates and garnish them with the sautéed morels. At Tribeca Grill, the polenta is served alongside the squab as "quenelles," molded into small egg shapes using two dessert spoons. It makes an attractive presentation with the squab.

TRIBECA GRILL · WARM CASHEW *FINANCIER* WITH FROZEN MASCARPONE MOUSSE, COFFEE ANGLAISE, CHOCOLATE SAUCE & CANDIED CASHEWS

THE INDIVIDUAL COMPONENTS of this dessert should be prepared in advance, as they are by Chef McKirday in the kitchen of Tribeca Grill. The mousse can be stored in the freezer for up to one month, the coffee anglaise, chocolate sauce, and candied cashews can be prepared early in the day and kept at room temperature. The *financier* batter must chill for at least one hour before baking, and the cake can be prepared one full day in advance. By reducing the recipe to its individual components, you can bring this elegant and complicated dessert to the table quite easily. (If you don't have 12 ramekins, you may wish to begin by making the mousse to free up the ramekins for the *financiers.*)

SERVES SIX

The mousse
1/4 cup sugar
2 tablespoons water
1/4 teaspoon fresh lemon juice
1 egg white
8 ounces mascarpone, at room temperature

The financier
1 cup unsalted butter
2/3 cup cashews
1 1/2 cups confectioners' sugar
2/3 cup cake flour
2 tablespoons cocoa powder
5 egg whites

The coffee Anglaise
1 cup milk
3 egg yolks
1/4 cup sugar
1 teaspoon instant coffee
ice

The chocolate sauce
4 tablespoons heavy cream
4 ounces bittersweet chocolate

The candied cashews
20 roasted cashews
1 tablespoon molasses
confectioners' sugar
bittersweet chocolate for garnish

To Prepare the Mousse: Place the sugar, water, and lemon juice in a small nonreactive saucepan, and stir to moisten all of the sugar. Heat at a medium temperature until it reaches 230 degrees on a candy thermometer. Continue cooking. Meanwhile, beat the egg white, using an electric mixer, until it is white and frothy.

When the syrup reaches 248 degrees, remove the pan from the heat and pour the syrup slowly down the inside of the bowl of egg white while you mix it at high speed. When you have added all of the syrup, reduce the mixer speed to medium and continue beating until the bowl is just warm to the touch.

In a large mixing bowl, beat the mascarpone lightly with a wire whisk. Beat one-third of the egg-white mixture into the mascarpone until it is incorporated. Fold in the remaining egg-white mixture. Spoon the mousse into six 4-ounce ramekins, filling them only halfway. Level the surface of each one with the back of a rubber spatula. Place the ramekins in the freezer for at least 1 1/2 hours.

To loosen the mousse from the ramekin, insert a warm knife around the edge. If necessary, briefly dip the ramekin in a shallow warm water bath. Invert each ramekin onto a flat surface.

To Prepare the Financiers: Cook the butter in a medium-sized saucepan over a medium to low heat until it is melted and lightly browned. (It will have a nutty aroma.) Pass it through a fine sieve to remove the fatty solids. Or let it cool slightly until the solids settle, and pour off the usable butter from the top.

Place the cashews in the bowl of a food processor with 1/2 cup of the confectioners' sugar and process. Set aside. Sift together the flour, cocoa, and remaining 1 cup of confectioners' sugar in a large mixing bowl. Add the ground cashew mixture and toss to combine. Add the egg whites, one at a time, and mix until the ingredients are fully incorporated. Slowly add the butter, with the mixer speed set at low.

Preheat the oven to 350 degrees. Butter six 4-ounce ramekins. Distribute the batter evenly among the ramekins, and bake for 25 minutes, until the tops of the cakes are golden. Remove the cakes from the ramekins immediately, and place them on a wire rack to cool.

To Make the Coffee Anglaise: Heat the milk in a saucepan over medium heat until it is hot but not boiling. Meanwhile, beat the egg yolks and sugar together in a small mixing bowl until the mixture is pale yellow. Pour the heated milk over the egg-yolk mixture and stir. Pass this mixture through a fine sieve back into the saucepan. Add the instant coffee and cook the mixture over medium heat, stirring constantly with a wooden spoon until the mixture is thick enough to coat the back of the spoon. Remove the pan to an ice bath. When the sauce has cooled to room temperature, transfer it to a covered dish. Serve the sauce at room temperature.

To Make the Chocolate Sauce: Heat the cream in a small saucepan over medium heat until it is hot but not boiling. Remove from the heat. Add the chocolate and stir it into the cream as it melts. Serve the sauce at room temperature. (If you make the sauce in advance, you may wish to reheat it before serving in order to thin it a bit.)

To Make the Candied Cashews: Toss the cashews and molasses in a small nonreactive bowl. Pour the cashews onto a baking sheet or a sheet of waxed paper. Dust them with confectioners' sugar. Set aside to use as garnish. (These will keep for a few hours at room temperature.)

To Assemble: Remove the ramekins from the freezer 1 hour before serving and place them in the refrigerator. Preheat the oven to 300 degrees. Warm the *financiers* for 5 minutes. Remove from the oven. Place each *financier* on a dessert plate. Top each one with a mascarpone mousse. Spoon some of the coffee anglaise around the *financier*. Spoon some of the chocolate sauce over the coffee anglaise. Garnish the dessert plates with candied cashews and chocolate shavings.

TWO ELEVEN RESTAURANT

211 WEST BROADWAY, NEW YORK, N.Y. 925-7202

TWO ELEVEN RESTAURANT

Spring Menu

PORTOBELLO & OYSTER MUSHROOMS WITH HERBED GOATS' MILK CHEESE IN PUFF PASTRY

GRILLED CHICKEN BREASTS WITH OREGANO BUTTER, WARM WILD RICE SALAD & SAUTÉED MUSTARD GREENS

ORANGE CRÈME BRÛLÉE

PORTOBELLO & OYSTER MUSHROOMS WITH HERBED GOATS' MILK CHEESE IN PUFF PASTRY

NOW THAT PUFF pastry is a staple in the grocer's freezer, this is a simple dish to prepare. You may alter the variety of mushrooms used, depending on what is fresh, but portobello and oyster mushrooms are available most of the year. Both the puff pastry and the mushrooms can be prepared early in the day. Assemble and cook the pastries as your guests come to the table.

SERVES EIGHT

10 x 10 inch sheet puff
   pastry, frozen
2 tablespoons olive oil
1 pound portobello mushrooms caps, sliced 1/4 inch thick
1 pound oyster mushrooms, stems removed and coarsely chopped
4 shallots, finely chopped
2 cloves garlic, minced
2 tablespoons fresh herbs (such as flat-leaf parsley, chives, oregano, or rosemary), chopped
4 ounces goats' milk cheese

To Prepare the Pastry: Cut four 5-inch squares of puff pastry. Then cut each square in half diagonally. With a small sharp knife, score a concentric triangle inside each puff pastry triangle, 1/2 inch in from the edges. (The inner triangle will serve as a pastry lid in the final presentation.)

Preheat the oven to 350 degrees. Transfer the pastry triangles to a parchment-covered baking sheet, and place the baking sheet in the freezer for 10 minutes. Remove from the freezer. Bake the pastry triangles for about 10 minutes, or until they are puffy and brown. (Watch them carefully so they don't burn.) Remove from the oven and place the triangles on a wire rack to cool. When they are completely cool, carefully lift out the inner triangle from each pastry. If there is any soggy pastry inside, remove it with your fingers and discard. Do not refrigerate the puff pastry once it is baked, because it will lose its crispness.

†WINE SUGGESTION

Tom Oliva, general manager at Two Eleven, recommends the following wines to be served with this menu: with the Portobello & Oyster Mushrooms in Puff Pastry a 1990 Hugel Riesling from Alsace; with the Grilled Chicken Breasts a 1990 E. Guigal Côtes du Rhône; and with the Orange Crème Brûlée a Colosi Malvasia della Lipani "Passito."

To Prepare the Filling: Heat the olive oil in a sauté pan over high heat. Add the mushrooms and sauté them quickly, turning them frequently so they sear evenly on all sides. Add the shallots and garlic and continue to sauté until the mushrooms are cooked. Remove from the heat. Stir in the chopped herbs and set aside.

To Assemble: Preheat the oven to 350 degrees. Crumble the cheese and divide it evenly among the triangle bottoms, reserving some cheese to sprinkle on top. Generously fill the pastries with the mushroom filling and sprinkle the reserved cheese on top. Bake for 5 minutes, or until the cheese is slightly melted and the mushrooms are warm. Cover the triangles with their pastry lids. Return the baking sheet to the oven to warm the triangles for 3 more minutes. Serve immediately.

TWO ELEVEN RESTAURANT GRILLED CHICKEN BREASTS WITH OREGANO BUTTER, WARM WILD RICE SALAD & SAUTÉED MUSTARD GREENS

THIS DISH OFFERS a wide range of textures, colors, and flavors to tempt the eye and the palate. The oregano-flavored butter melted over the simply grilled chicken provides complex flavoring with ease of preparation. Prepare the oregano butter in advance. You can store it in the refrigerator for up to three days. Be sure to let it sit at room temperature for about an hour before serving. The wild rice can also be made in advance and reheated in the oven, covered. Add one-half cup of chicken

stock to the rice so it doesn't dry out. Reheat it in a 300-degree oven for about 10 minutes. With the rice salad and oregano butter made in advance, you can time the dish just right if you sauté the mustard greens while the chicken is grilling; both take about ten minutes to cook.

SERVES EIGHT

The oregano butter
I cup butter, softened
juice of I/2 lime
I/2 cup red onion, minced
I/2 cup fresh parsley, finely chopped
I/2 cup fresh oregano, chopped
I/2 teaspoon salt
2 teaspoons freshly ground pepper

The wild rice salad
2 cups wild rice
4 cups water
I/2 medium-sized carrot, peeled
I stalk celery
I small yellow onion, halved
I teaspoon salt
3/4 cup fresh orange juice
I small red onion, finely diced
I/2 cup fresh mint, finely chopped
I cup fresh cilantro or parsley,
    finely chopped
I/2 cup sliced almonds, toasted

The chicken
8 boneless chicken breasts
salt
freshly ground pepper

The mustard greens
I/4 cup olive oil
2 shallots, minced
2 pounds mustard greens, washed

To Make the Oregano Butter: Combine the butter, lime juice, onions, parsley, oregano, salt, and pepper in the bowl of a food processor. Blend thoroughly. On a large piece of plastic wrap, form the butter into a tube shape, about 2 inches in diameter and 8 inches long. Store it in the refrigerator until one hour before serving.

To Make the Wild Rice Salad: Combine the rice, water, carrot, celery, yellow onion, and salt in a 4-quart saucepan. Bring the water to a boil, cover, and lower the heat. Simmer for about I hour, or until the rice is tender. Remove the pan from the heat. Discard the carrot, celery, and onion, and pour off any excess water. Stir in the orange juice, red onions, mint, cilantro, and toasted almonds. Cover to keep warm.

To Grill the Chicken: Prepare the grill. Season the chicken breasts with salt and pepper. Grill the chicken for about 10 minutes. (After 5 minutes, turn each chicken breast to cook the other side.) Meanwhile, prepare the mustard greens.

To Cook the Mustard Greens: Heat the olive oil and shallots in a large sauté pan over medium-high heat for 3 minutes. Add the mustard greens and cook them for 7 minutes, stirring occasionally.

To Serve: Place two generous spoonfuls of warm wild rice salad on each of 8 warm dinner plates. Top each bed of rice with a grilled chicken breast and place a 1-inch portion of compound butter on the chicken. Surround the rice with mustard greens.

TWO ELEVEN
RESTAURANT

ORANGE CRÈME BRÛLÉE

THE SIMPLE ADDITION of orange juice and zest makes this crème brûlée special. The custard will keep in the refrigerator for several days, so this is certainly a dessert that can be made in advance. Don't caramelize the tops too far in advance or the sugar will break down with moisture. However, plan on chilling the dessert for at least an hour after caramelizing the tops so the custard has a chance to reset.

SERVES EIGHT

The custard
1 1/2 cups heavy cream
1/3 cup milk
7 egg yolks
1/2 cup sugar
2 tablespoons orange zest (from 2 to 3 oranges)
1/4 cup fresh orange juice
3 tablespoons Triple Sec

The brûlée topping
1/2 cup sugar

Preheat the oven to 325 degrees. In a heavy saucepan, combine the cream and milk and bring the liquid just to the boil. Meanwhile, whisk together the egg yolks and sugar in a nonreactive bowl. When the cream and milk have reached a boil, slowly whisk the hot liquid into the egg-yolk mixture. Pour the custard through a fine sieve back into the saucepan to strain out any bits of curdled egg. Whisk in the orange zest, orange juice, and Triple Sec.

Divide the custard equally among eight 4-ounce ramekins. Place the filled ramekins on a jelly-roll pan or other large baking dish. Pour hot water around the ramekins to a depth of 1 inch. Bake the custards in this water bath for 35 to 40 minutes, or until the custard is set. (The custards are done when a sharp knife inserted near the edge comes out clean.) Allow the custards to cool in the water bath. Then refrigerate for at least two hours.

To Make the Topping: Remove the ramekins from the refrigerator. Sprinkle 1 tablespoon of sugar on top of each custard. Place the ramekins under the broiler and cook for about 3 minutes, or until the sugar turns a deep brown. (Watch carefully so the sugar doesn't burn.) Remove from the oven quickly. (The edges will be darker than the center and the sugar will continue to cook for a while.) Allow the tops to cool. Then return the ramekins to the refrigerator until ready to serve.

SUMMER

ARQUA

Summer Menu

❧

SAFFRON
RISOTTO CAKES
WITH CHEESE &
VEGETABLE
RELISH

VITELLO
TONNATO

WHITE
PEACHES WITH
PROSECO

SAFFRON RISOTTO CAKES WITH CHEESE & VEGETABLE RELISH

THE VEGETABLE relish for this dish is a visual treat and a taste celebration of summer. The risotto cakes must be assembled and chilled at least one hour in advance. They can be refrigerated for up to six hours before the final preparation.

SERVES SIX

Risotto cakes
10 threads saffron
1 quart chicken stock
1 tablespoon olive oil
1/2 medium onion, finely chopped
2 1/2 cups Arborio rice
1/2 cup dry white wine
8 ounces robiola, mascarpone, or cream cheese
1/2 cup olive oil (for frying)
flour

Vegetable relish
8 ripe plum tomatoes, seeded
1 whole cucumber, peeled and seeded
1 each green, yellow, and red bell pepper
1 medium red onion
8 to 10 fresh basil leaves, chopped
1/2 cup olive oil
1 tablespoon lemon juice
salt
freshly ground pepper

To Make the Risotto Cakes: Dissolve the saffron in the chicken stock in a saucepan over medium heat. Remove from the heat and set aside. Heat the olive oil in a large saucepan at a medium-high temperature. Sear the onions for 2 to 3 minutes, being careful not to burn them. Stir in the rice and wine and let the wine evaporate. Lower the heat and add enough chicken stock to cover the rice. Stir until the rice absorbs the stock. Then add the remaining chicken stock all at once and cook for 15 to 20 minutes, or until the rice is cooked most of the way but is still firm. Stir occasionally while it is cooking. Remove from the heat and place the pan in a bowl of ice water until the rice is cool.

†WINE SUGGESTION

Leo Pulito, proprietor and chef of Arqua, recommends serving a Verdicchio di Jesi, 1991 or 1992, preferably produced by Fratelli Bucci, to accompany both the Saffron Risotto Cakes and the Vitello Tonnato. He also recommends using a Proseco from the Conegliano area of Italy to accompany and to prepare the White Peaches.

Form the rice into 6 balls and cut each one in half. Flatten each shape to make a 4-inch patty. Place a spoonful of cheese in the center of one patty. Cover it with another patty and seal the edges carefully, keeping the cheese in the middle. Repeat until you have 6 cheese-filled rice cakes. Cover the cakes in plastic wrap and refrigerate them for 1 to 6 hours.

Heat the olive oil in a large sauté pan at a medium-high temperature. Dust the cakes with flour on both sides and fry them until they are golden brown. Blot the cakes on a paper towel. Serve warm.

To Make the Vegetable Relish: Dice the tomatoes, cucumber, bell peppers, and onion into 1/4-inch pieces. Combine the vegetables with the basil, olive oil, lemon juice, salt, and pepper in a small nonreactive bowl. Allow the relish to sit for at least 15 minutes but not more than 4 hours. Serve at room temperature.

To Serve: Chef Pulito recommends serving each risotto cake in the center of a large plate surrounded by the vegetable relish.

ARQUA VITELLO TONNATO

THIS CLASSIC ITALIAN summer dish is a delight to prepare and present, especially because you can cook the meat and prepare the sauce up to four days in advance. The most important ingredient for a successful vitello tonnato is the cut of veal. Ask the butcher for an eye round, top round, or loin cut. The cut is important not only to guarantee the finest flavor but also to ensure that the meat can be thinly sliced without falling apart. Chef Pulito prefers to use salt-packed capers for the garnish. If you are using brine-packed capers, be sure to drain them well.

SERVES SIX

Veal roast
1 1/2 pounds veal
salt
freshly ground pepper

I/2 cup olive oil
I/2 cup dry white wine
I/2 cup chicken stock

The sauce
I egg
pinch of salt
pinch of freshly ground white pepper
5 oil-packed anchovy fillets, drained
I I/2 teaspoons lemon juice
I/2 cup olive oil
I 6-ounce can white tuna packed in olive oil, not
    drained
capers for garnish

To Prepare the Veal: Preheat the oven to 425
degrees. Season the veal with salt and pepper.
Heat the olive oil in a large ovenproof sauté pan
at a high temperature. When the oil is hot, add
the veal and brown it on all sides. Splash the
wine over the veal and continue cooking over a
medium-high heat until the wine is reduced by
half. Stir to loosen any meat from the bottom of
the pan. Add the chicken stock and remove the
pan from the heat. Roast the veal for 15 minutes (medium-rare on the meat thermometer).
Remove the pan from the oven and allow the
veal to cool. Wrap and refrigerate the meat until
chilled, or up to 4 days.

To Make the Sauce: Place the egg, salt, pepper,
anchovy fillets, and I/2 teaspoon of the lemon
juice in the bowl of a food processor and blend.
Add the olive oil in a slow stream while the food
processor is running. Add the tuna and the

remaining lemon juice and purée. Transfer the
sauce to an airtight container and refrigerate
until chilled.

To Serve: Cut the veal into thin slices—ideally,
about I/I6 inch thick. Arrange the slices on a
serving platter and pour the chilled sauce over the
veal. Garnish with capers.

ARQUA
WHITE PEACHES
WITH PROSECO

TRY ADDING A few fresh raspberries to each
glass to bring a burst of color to this refreshing and
simple but elegant dessert.

SERVES SIX

6 ripe medium-sized white peaches
I tablespoon lemon juice
I/4 cup sugar
I split of Proseco or other dry white sparkling
    wine, chilled

Peel the peaches and cut them into I-inch wedges.
Transfer the peaches to a nonreactive bowl and toss
them with the lemon juice and sugar. Allow them to
sit for 20 minutes.

    Divide the peaches equally among 6 open-
mouthed stemmed glasses. Slowly pour an equal
amount of Proseco (or other sparkling wine) into
each glass, being careful not to let it overflow.
Place each glass on a dessert plate and serve
immediately.

CHANTERELLE

Summer Menu

SALAD OF MAINE
CRAB WITH
HEARTS OF PALM

SAUTÉ OF
CHICKEN WITH
PARSLEY,
TOMATO &
GARLIC

CORN CUSTARD

PLUM *CLAFOUTI*

SALAD OF MAINE CRAB WITH HEARTS OF PALM

THIS LIGHT, COLORFUL dish is full of fresh flavors. It is simple to make and, once all of the ingredients are on hand, it goes together quickly. You may substitute Maryland crab or canned crabmeat for the Maine crab, and canned hearts of palm for fresh.

SERVES SIX

The dressing
1/4 cup extra virgin olive oil
2 tablespoons fresh lime juice
2 tablespoons finely chopped fresh cilantro
2 tablespoons finely chopped fresh mint
1/2 clove garlic, coarsely chopped
salt
freshly ground pepper

The salad
1/2 pound Mesclun greens or any assortment of fresh lettuce
1/2 pound hearts of palm, julienned into 2 x 1/8 inch strips
12 ounces cooked Maine crabmeat, chilled
edible flowers (such as nasturtiums, marigolds, or pansies) for garnish

To Make the Dressing: Combine the olive oil, lime juice, cilantro, mint, and garlic in the bowl of a food processor and purée. Season with salt and pepper, and add more lime juice if necessary. Set the dressing aside.

To Serve: Arrange the Mesclun greens on 6 individual salad plates. In a small nonreactive bowl, toss the hearts of palm with one-fourth of the dressing, and place them over the greens. Then toss the crabmeat with one-fourth of the dressing and place it on top of the hearts of palm. Spoon the remaining dressing over the salads and garnish with the edible flowers. Serve.

Chanterelle

2 Harrison Street
New York City, New York
10013

(212) 966-6960

†WINE SUGGESTION

World-class sommelier Roger Dagorn has added his suggestions for pairing wines with the recipes that Chef David Waltuck has chosen for this summer menu. To start, serve a Condrieu, Château du Rozay, 1990; for the main course, Chinon Varennes du Grand Clos, Charles Joguet de la Dioterie, 1988; and with dessert, Jurançon Moelleux, Domaine Cauhapé, Quintessence du Petit-Manseng, 1990.

SAUTÉ OF CHICKEN WITH PARSLEY, TOMATO & GARLIC

THIS IS A very comforting chicken dish with a full, fresh flavor. Chef Waltuck recommends serving it with fettuccine or rice. The quality of tomato will make a difference in the sauce. Choose ripe, farm-fresh tomatoes at their finest. This recipe calls for three whole chickens cut into parts. You may prefer to buy the chickens already cut up. In this case, buy about 7 1/2 pounds of chicken breasts, thighs, and legs.

SERVES SIX

3 2 1/2-pound chickens, cut up into parts
   (reserve wings and backs for stock)
salt
freshly ground pepper
3/4 cup clarified butter
6 cloves garlic, coarsely chopped
2 cups fresh tomatoes—blanched, peeled, seeded,
   and diced
1/4 cup brandy
1 tablespoon tomato paste
1 1/2 cups heavy cream
2 tablespoons fresh lemon juice
1/2 cup flat-leaf parsley, coarsely chopped

Season the chicken parts lightly with salt and pepper. Heat the clarified butter in a heavy sauté pan over high heat and add the chicken legs and thighs. Brown them well on all sides and transfer them to an 8-quart casserole. Then brown the chicken breasts on all sides in the same sauté pan. Transfer them to the casserole with the legs and thighs. Set aside.

Discard all but 3 tablespoons of the fat from the sauté pan. Lower the heat and brown the garlic very lightly in the fat. Add the tomatoes, brandy, and tomato paste and simmer for 2 minutes. Add the heavy cream and bring the mixture to a boil. Remove from the heat. Pour the mixture over the chicken pieces. Set aside the sauté pan but don't wash it yet.

Flowers at Chanterelle

Place the casserole over a medium-low heat. Simmer for 10 to 15 minutes, moving the chicken pieces around occasionally. (If the white-meat pieces are thoroughly cooked after 10 minutes, transfer them to a serving platter and keep them warm. Continue cooking the dark-meat pieces for about 5 minutes, until they are thoroughly cooked.) Transfer the chicken pieces to a serving platter and keep them warm. Pour the sauce back into the sauté pan.

Cook the sauce over medium-high heat, stirring constantly, for 3 to 5 minutes, or until it is thick. Season the sauce with lemon juice, salt, and pepper. Pour the sauce over the chicken pieces and sprinkle the chopped parsley on top. Serve immediately.

CHANTERELLE CORN CUSTARD

THIS VEGETABLE DISH is very pleasing and simple to prepare. Enjoy it year-round by using frozen corn, but the dish is at its best with fresh, sweet summer corn cut from the cob. These custards may be cooked one day ahead. Leave them in the ramekins and reheat them in a water bath in a 250-degree oven. Then turn them out to serve.

SERVES SIX

6 ears of corn, shucked (or 5 cups frozen
  corn kernels)
3 eggs
3/4 cup heavy cream
I dash each salt, pepper, cayenne pepper,
  and nutmeg

Drop the ears of corn in a large pot of boiling water and leave for I minute. Remove and immediately plunge them into cold water. Cut the kernels from the cobs. (If you are using

frozen corn, cook it for only half the usual amount of time.) Set aside.

Butter six 4-ounce ramekins. Preheat the oven to 325 degrees. Purée the corn using a food processor. Pass it through a food mill into a large mixing bowl. (You should have I 1/2 cups of corn purée.) Add the eggs and cream and mix well. Add the salt, pepper, cayenne, and nutmeg.

Pour the purée into the buttered ramekins. Cover each one with aluminum foil and place the ramekins in a large baking dish filled halfway with water. Bake the custards about 45 minutes or until a knife inserted near the edge comes out clean. Remove the ramekins from the water bath and place them on a rack to cool slightly. Run a clean sharp knife around the inside edge of each ramekin. Invert the ramekin on an individual plate and gently rap on the bottom of it until the custard comes out. Handle the custards carefully, because they are fragile.

CHANTERELLE PLUM *CLAFOUTI*

THE PASTRY IN this dessert has the flavor and
texture of an excellent shortbread. The *clafouti* can
be made earlier in the day and served at room
temperature.

MAKES ONE 10-INCH TART

The pastry
1/2 cup cold butter
1 1/4 cups flour
1/2 cup sugar
1 egg, lightly beaten
baking weights or 2 cups dried beans

The filling
2 eggs
1/2 cup sugar
1/4 cup plus 2 tablespoons flour
1/4 cup plus 2 tablespoons heavy cream
1 tablespoon brandy
3 medium plums, pitted

To Make the Pastry: Cut the butter into 8 to 10 pieces
and place them in the bowl of a food processor.
Add the flour and sugar. Process using the pulse
button 5 or 6 times. Add the beaten egg to the
butter mixture and process using the pulse button
until the mixture resembles coarse meal. Scrape the
dough onto a sheet of plastic wrap. Form it into a
flattened ball and refrigerate it for 1 hour.

Preheat the oven to 350 degrees. Using your
fingers and the heel of your palm, press the chilled
dough evenly into the bottom and along the sides
of a 10-inch tart pan that has a removable bottom.

Line the tart shell with waxed paper or parchment paper cut to about 15 inches in diameter. Fill
the shell with baking weights or beans, and bake it
for about 15 minutes, or until the dough has just
begun to color slightly. Remove the tart shell from
the oven and allow it to cool for 5 minutes. Remove
the weights or beans and the paper.

To Make the Filling: Combine the eggs with the sugar,
flour, cream, and brandy in a medium-sized mixing
bowl. Blend thoroughly with an electric mixer. Set
aside. Cut each plum into 10 to 12 equal-sized
wedges. Arrange the plum wedges in two tightly
formed concentric circles in the tart shell. Pour the
custard mixture over the plums. Bake the tart for
35 to 40 minutes, or until the crust and custard
are golden brown. Remove from the oven. Allow
the tart to cool. Serve at room temperature.

COOKBOOK

PANZANELLA WITH MIXED FIELD GREENS

Panzanella is a dish of Tuscan origin that turns leftover bread into an appetizer that sets the taste buds into action. The higher the quality of oil and vinegar, the better the salad. Use well-dried bread that can absorb the dressing without falling apart. You will need about three cups of bread for this recipe. If you don't have any leftover bread, then you can cut up a fresh loaf and dry it in a warm place for a few hours before making the salad. Or cut the bread into cubes and bake them at 300 degrees for about 5 minutes, being careful not to toast the bread.

SERVES SIX

DUANE PARK CAFE

Summer Menu

PANZANELLA WITH MIXED FIELD GREENS

VEAL WITH SWEET VERMOUTH, SAGE & PROSCIUTTO

POTATO SALAD WITH MUSHROOMS & SUN-DRIED TOMATOES

WHITE PEACH GRANITA WITH RASPBERRIES, ZABAGLIONE & ALMOND BISCOTTI

✝WINE SUGGESTION

General Manager Alfred A. Chiodo recommends serving a selection of Italian wines with this menu. A Castel San Valentino Pinot Grigio, 1993, from Alto Adige to accompany the Panzanella with Mixed Field Greens; a Clerico Dolcetto d'Alda, 1992, from Piedmont to accompany the Veal with Sweet Vermouth, Sage & Prosciutto; and a Moscato d'Asti, 1993, from Cascinetta to accompany the White Peach Granita.

SUMMER 73

1/4 cup balsamic vinegar

3/4 cup olive oil

1 1/2 teaspoons salt

1 large loaf of day-old thick-crusted bread

4 ripe tomatoes, seeded and chopped

2 small red onions, chopped

2 cloves garlic, minced

1/2 cup basil leaves, chopped

1/2 teaspoon freshly ground black pepper

6 large handfuls Mesclun (or a variety of unusual lettuce, especially bitter greens), washed and dried

To Make the Vinaigrette: Whisk together the vinegar, olive oil, and 1/2 teaspoon of salt. Set aside.

To Make the Salad: Remove the crust from the bread. Tear the bread into pieces and let them dry out. Meanwhile, combine the tomatoes, onions, garlic, basil, pepper, and the remaining teaspoon of salt in a medium-sized nonreactive bowl, and let the mixture sit at room temperature for 30 minutes.

To Serve: Toss the bread with the tomato mixture. Then toss half of the vinaigrette with the bread mixture and the other half with the lettuce, placed in a large bowl. Distribute the lettuce among 6 salad plates and top with equal amounts of the bread-and-tomato mixture.

DUANE PARK CAFE

VEAL WITH SWEET VERMOUTH, SAGE & PROSCIUTTO

THIS SIMPLE DISH is delicious made with veal chops, but you may also use veal steaks. Purchase a whole loin of veal or veal roast and have the butcher cut it into one-inch steaks. This dish requires very little preparation, and the final cooking process takes only 15 minutes.

SERVES SIX

1/4 cup olive oil

6 veal chops

2 cloves garlic, finely chopped

6 large fresh sage leaves, chopped, or 1 teaspoon dried sage

3 slices prosciutto or other dry Italian-style ham, cut into strips

1 cup sweet red vermouth

1/2 teaspoon salt

1/2 teaspoon freshly ground pepper

additional whole sage leaves and prosciutto strips for garnish (optional)

Heat the olive oil in a heavy skillet over high heat. Sear the veal chops for 3 minutes on each side. Transfer them to a warm platter and keep them warm.

Drain the excess oil from the pan and add the garlic, sage, and prosciutto. Cook these ingredients over medium-high heat for 30 seconds. Then add the vermouth, stirring to

release any browned bits of meat from the pan. Add the salt and pepper. Return the veal chops to the pan, reduce the heat, and simmer for 3 minutes. (Turn the chops over once.) Remove from the heat.

To Serve: Place the veal chops on warm dinner plates and pour the reduced liquid over them. Garnish with additional sage leaves and prosciutto strips. Serve immediately.

DUANE PARK CAFE

POTATO SALAD WITH MUSHROOMS & SUN-DRIED TOMATOES

CHEF MAEDA RECOMMENDS tossing the potatoes in the vinaigrette while they are still hot. This allows the potatoes to absorb the vinaigrette and gives the salad a unique flavor. However, you can make the entire salad a day in advance and keep it in the refrigerator; return it to room temperature before serving. For this recipe, try to use sun-dried tomatoes that are dry, not packed in oil. If you can only find the oil-packed kind, be sure to drain them completely, rinse them, and pat them dry before using.

SERVES SIX

The dressing
1 cup extra virgin olive oil
1/4 cup balsamic vinegar
1 teaspoon salt
1/2 teaspoon freshly ground black pepper

The potatoes
3 pounds new potatoes, scrubbed clean
pinch of salt

The tomatoes and mushrooms
12 sun-dried tomatoes
12 mushrooms, cleaned and thickly sliced
2 tablespoons olive oil
1 tablespoon fresh sage, chopped
1 clove garlic, minced
3/4 cup chopped parsley

To Make the Dressing: In a large nonreactive bowl, combine the olive oil, balsamic vinegar, salt, and pepper. Whisk these ingredients to blend them well. Set aside.

To Prepare the Potatoes: Cut the potatoes into 2-inch pieces. Place them in cold, salted water. Bring the water to a boil and continue cooking the potatoes for about 10 minutes, or until they are tender but still firm. Remove from the heat. Drain the potatoes. Pat them dry with paper towels, and toss them in a large bowl with the vinaigrette. Set aside to cool.

To Prepare the Tomatoes and Mushrooms: Drop the sun-dried tomatoes in boiling water and leave them for 2 minutes. Drain them immediately and chop them. Set aside.

Sauté the mushrooms in the oil for about 5 minutes. Remove from the heat and stir in the sage, garlic, parsley, and tomatoes. Add these ingredients to the potatoes and toss well. Serve at room temperature.

DUANE PARK CAFE

WHITE PEACH GRANITA WITH RASPBERRIES, ZABAGLIONE & ALMOND BISCOTTI

FOR THIS DESSERT, Chef Maeda uses frozen white-peach purée. He recommends using this ingredient if you can find it. (You will need one 34-ounce package.) You can also make your own purée according to the directions below. Or you may simply thaw frozen yellow peaches and purée them using a food processor. Each component of this recipe can be prepared in advance, in stages. The peach granita will keep in the freezer for a few months, stored in a covered container. The *biscotti*, which have a

peppery zing to them, will keep in an airtight container for at least a week. The zabaglione can be prepared a few hours before serving and stored in a covered container in the refrigerator. Chef Maeda recommends serving this dessert in chilled red wine glasses. This way, your guests can appreciate the wonderful blend of colors in this layered summertime dessert.

SERVES SIX

The peach granita
8 1/2 cups peeled, sliced white peaches
juice of 1 lemon
1/4 cup kirsch

The biscotti
1/2 cup butter, softened to room temperature
1 cup granulated sugar
2 eggs
zest of 1 lemon
zest of 1 orange
1 1/2 teaspoons vanilla extract
1/2 teaspoon almond extract
2 cups flour
1/2 teaspoon baking powder
1/8 teaspoon salt
1 1/2 teaspoons black pepper

1 cup sliced almonds, ground to resemble
   coarse meal
1 cup whole almonds

The zabaglione and berries
8 egg yolks
1/4 cup sugar
3/4 cup white wine
zest of 1 orange
zest of 1 lemon
4 tablespoons orange liqueur
1/4 teaspoon nutmeg
1/2 cup heavy cream
2 pints fresh raspberries

To Prepare the Granita: Purée the peaches in a food processor in batches. Add the lemon juice and kirsch and process until well blended. Pour the purée into a jelly-roll pan and place it in the freezer. Stir the purée occasionally with a fork until it freezes. If you are not using the granita immediately, transfer it to a plastic container and store it, covered, in the freezer for up to 2 months.

To Make the Biscotti: Cream the butter in the bowl of an electric mixer. Add the sugar and eggs and mix until fluffy. Scrape the bowl and add the zest and the vanilla and almond extracts, and mix until smooth.

   In a separate bowl, sift together the flour, baking powder, salt, and pepper. Add the ground almonds and the whole almonds, and toss gently to combine. Stir the dry ingredients into the butter mixture. Line a baking sheet with parchment paper, or butter the baking sheet. Turn out the dough on a lightly floured surface and form it into a long shape, about 1 1/2 inches thick.

Transfer the dough onto the baking sheet and place it in the refrigerator for 30 minutes.

   Preheat the oven to 325 degrees. Remove the baking sheet from the refrigerator. Bake the biscotti about 30 to 40 minutes, or until lightly browned. Remove from the oven and cool briefly. (Leave the oven on.) When the biscotti is cool to the touch, cut it on a diagonal into 1/2-inch-thick slices using a serrated knife. Arrange these slices, spaced apart, on two baking sheets, and bake them for 15 minutes. (Halfway through the baking time, turn the biscotti so they will brown evenly.) Remove from the oven, and place the biscotti on a wire rack to cool. Store them in a tightly sealed cookie tin.

To Prepare the Zabaglione: Combine the egg yolks and sugar in a medium-sized nonreactive bowl, and beat using an electric mixer until the mixture is thick, pale yellow, and airy. Transfer this mixture to a double boiler and continue beating with a whisk while adding the wine, orange and lemon zest, liqueur, and nutmeg. Cook the custard over boiling water, whisking constantly, until it becomes foamy and then thickens. Immediately remove from the heat and plunge the pan into an ice bath, continuing to stir until the custard cools. Leave it in the ice bath to chill completely.

   Meanwhile, beat the cream in a small bowl, using an electric mixer, until it is stiff. Fold the whipped cream into the chilled custard. Return the zabaglione to the ice bath until you are ready to serve it. Or transfer it to a serving dish and store it, covered, in the refrigerator.

To Serve: Spoon the granita into 6 large chilled wine glasses. Top the granita with zabaglione and fresh raspberries. Serve with biscotti.

EL TEDDY'S

*A Four-Course
Tasting Menu*

❧

Mexican Buffet

MARGARITAS

*TOSTADAS DE
CAMARÓNES*

YUCATÁN
GRILLED STEAK,
CHICKEN BREASTS
& WHOLE RED
SNAPPER

*PICO DE GALLO,
AVOCADO SAUCE
& SALSA PICANTE*

ARROZ VERDE

*TORTA DE TRES
LECHES*

MARGARITAS

AN AUTHENTIC
Mexican barbeque should
begin with margaritas, a
cool and refreshing cocktail.
Serve these with the appetizer, the *Tostadas de
Camarónes.*

SERVES EIGHT

16 ounces tequila
 (preferably Sauza
 Commemorativo)
8 ounces Triple Sec
8 ounces fresh lime juice
2 cups cracked ice
additional lime
 (optional)
kosher salt
 (optional)

Combine the tequila,
Triple Sec, and lime juice
in a cocktail shaker or a
large jar with a lid. Add the
cracked ice and shake vigorously. Pour the liquid
through a strainer into 8 large martini glasses. (If
you wish, prepare the glasses beforehand by rubbing a cut lime along each rim and dipping the
wet rim in kosher salt. Then fill the glasses.)

†WINE SUGGESTION

*Chef Peter Klein offers his recipe for margaritas and sug-
gests serving them throughout the meal.*

EL TEDDY'S

TOSTADAS DE CAMARÓNES

THIS COLORFUL DISH is light but still richly
flavorful. The beans call for a dried Mexican herb
called epazote. If you cannot find this herb, you
can substitute dried marjoram. Control the spici-
ness of the dish by adjusting the amount of chiles
and jalapeños. This recipe takes very little time to
cook and assemble. However, you will have to cook
the beans in advance. (See page 165 on cooking
dried beans.) Begin with two cups of dried beans.

SERVES EIGHT

The refried beans
4 cups cooked pinto beans (or black beans or
 kidney beans)
1 serrano chile, finely chopped
2 cloves garlic, minced
1 tablespoon epazote, or marjoram
1 teaspoon salt
pinch of white pepper
about 1 cup cooking liquid from beans
2 tablespoons olive oil

The tostadas
1 pound medium shrimp, peeled and deveined
 salt
freshly ground pepper
1 1/4 cups olive oil
2 pickled jalapeños, drained and finely chopped
2 ounces pickled onions, drained and finely
 chopped
4 sweet gherkins (pickles), finely chopped
1 head *frisée*, coarsely chopped

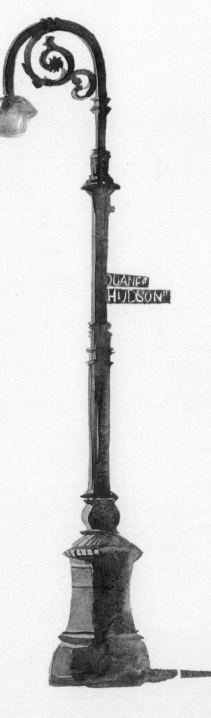

1 bunch watercress, rinsed and stemmed
1 ripe avocado, diced
1/4 cup lime juice
8 8-inch corn tortillas
corn oil for frying
6 ounces *queso blanco* or Monterey jack cheese, grated

To Prepare the Beans: Purée together the beans, chile, garlic, epazote, salt, and pepper. Add the cooking liquid as necessary for a smooth consistency. Set aside.

Heat the olive oil in a deep skillet over medium-high heat until the oil begins to smoke. Add the bean mixture all at once, stirring constantly. Lower the heat and cook for 4 minutes. Remove the pan from the heat and set it aside.

To Make the Tostadas: Season the shrimp with salt and pepper and sauté them in 1/4 cup of olive oil over medium heat until they are just cooked. (They should be opaque throughout.) Remove from the heat. Blot the shrimp with a paper towel and let them cool. Coarsely chop the shrimp and place them in a large bowl with the jalapeños, pickled onions, gherkins, frisée, watercress, avocado, lime juice, and the remaining 1 cup of olive oil. Toss these salad ingredients together and season with additional salt and pepper to taste. Set aside.

Fry the tortillas (on both sides) in the corn oil over high heat until they are crisp. Blot them on paper towels and set them aside.

To Assemble and Serve: Spread some of the bean mixture on one side of each fried tortilla. Sprinkle cheese over the bean mixture. Then distribute the salad mixture on top. Serve immediately.

EL TEDDY'S YUCATÁN GRILLED STEAK, CHICKEN BREASTS & WHOLE RED SNAPPER

THIS DISH IS a real crowd pleaser. You will be able to serve eight people very nicely with the recommended quantities given in this recipe. The chicken, meat, and fish are all delicious served just above room temperature, so there is some flexibility in the timing of the cooking of the three different meats. The chicken will take the longest time, followed by the fish, and then the steak. The achiote paste (made from annatto seeds) is available in specialty stores and by mail order (see the Sources Guide on page 165). Or you can make it according to the directions below. The paste will keep for one month in the refrigerator.

SERVES EIGHT

2-pound whole red snapper, scaled and gutted
   and gills removed
4 whole chicken breasts (with bone), split
1/2 cup achiote paste*
1/2 cup orange juice
1/2 cup olive oil
1 1/2 pounds flank or sirloin steak
cilantro for garnish
corn or flour tortillas, warmed

To Marinate the Meats: Rinse the fish and chicken under cold water and pat them dry. Set aside.

Whisk the achiote paste, orange juice, and olive oil together in a small bowl and rub the mixture generously over the fish, chicken, and steak. Place the meats (fish, chicken, and steak) in separate sealable plastic bags and refrigerate them for at least 2 hours, or overnight.

To Grill the Meats: Prepare the grill. Take the marinated meats from the refrigerator. Grill the chicken about 15 to 20 minutes (turning once). Grill the fish for about 10 to 15 minutes (turning once). Grill the steak for about 8 to 10 minutes (turning once). Let the steak stand for 5 to 10 minutes. Then slice it very thin.

To serve: Place the sliced steak, the chicken breasts, and the fish on separate serving platters and garnish them with cilantro. Serve the grilled meats with warm corn or flour tortillas and *Pico de Gallo*, Avocado Sauce, and *Salsa Picante* (see page 81).

*Achiote Paste
3 tablespoons ground annatto seeds
3 tablespoons finely chopped garlic
1 tablespoon oregano
3 tablespoons orange juice

Combine all of the ingredients in a food processor to make a paste.

EL TEDDY'S

PICO DE GALLO,
AVOCADO SAUCE, &
SALSA PICANTE

THESE THREE SAUCES are condiments for the Yucatán Grilled Steak, Chicken Breasts, & Whole Red Snapper. *Pico de Gallo* is a bright red, tomato-based sauce. Its name, loosely translated, means "rooster's cockscomb." The Avocado Sauce is a cool, soothing sauce. Make it close to serving time so the avocado doesn't have a chance to turn brown. Leave the avocado pit in the bowl as an added precaution against discoloration. The *Salsa Picante* is a spicy sauce. Adjust the flavor to suit your taste. We recommend placing the three sauces in decorative bowls among the serving platters on the buffet.

Pico de Gallo

10 ripe plum tomatoes, cored and diced small
1 small red onion, diced small
1/4 cup finely chopped cilantro
salt
white pepper

Avocado sauce

1 small clove garlic
1 small shallot
1 serrano chile
1 cup milk
1 ripe avocado
juice of 1 lime
1 tablespoon finely chopped cilantro
salt
pepper

Salsa Picante

1/2 pound tomatillos
1 medium red bell pepper—roasted, peeled, rinsed, and seeded
3 dried pequín peppers or 1 small chipotle pepper or 1/2 teaspoon hot pepper flakes
2 cloves garlic
salt

To Make the Pico de Gallo: Toss the tomatoes, onions, and cilantro together in a bowl and season with salt and pepper to taste. Allow the sauce to sit at least 30 minutes before serving.

To Make the Avocado Sauce: Place the garlic, shallot, chile, and milk in a blender. Blend until smooth. Peel the avocado. Remove the pit and reserve it. Place the avocado in the bowl of a food processor with the lime juice. Begin processing and slowly add the milk mixture. Process until smooth and then stir in the cilantro by hand. Season with salt and pepper.

To Make the Salsa Picante: Place the tomatillos in a bowl and cover them with hot tap water. Allow them to cool slightly. Then remove the husks, rinse the tomatillos clean, and cut each one in half. Place a couple of tomatillos in a blender and purée them. Add the remaining tomatillos, one at a time, alternating with the red bell pepper, the pequín peppers, and the garlic. Blend until smooth. Add salt to taste.

EL TEDDY'S · *ARROZ VERDE*

ARROZ VERDE, OR green rice, is a traditional Mexican side dish and a good accompaniment to the Yucatán Grilled Steak, Chicken Breasts & Whole Red Snapper. The rice should rest for 15 minutes after it has cooked. During this time you can grill the meat. Toast the almonds earlier in the day and keep them on a plate between two pieces of paper towel so they will stay crisp.

SERVES EIGHT

1/4 cup sliced almonds
1/2 cup cooked fresh or frozen spinach
1/2 cup loosely packed flat-leaf parsley, rinsed
    and stemmed
1 large clove garlic
1 shallot
2 1/4 cups water
salt
freshly ground pepper
1 tablespoon olive oil
2 1/4 cups converted white rice

Toast the almonds until they are golden brown. Set aside.

Squeeze any excess water from the spinach. Place the spinach in the bowl of a food processor, together with the parsley, garlic, shallot, and 1/4 cup of the water. Process until the mixture is smooth. Season to taste with salt and pepper.

Heat the olive oil in a large saucepan at a medium temperature and add the rice. Stir to coat the rice. Add the remaining 2 cups of water and the spinach mixture, stirring to combine. Bring the liquid to a boil. Cover the pan and reduce the heat to very low. Cook for 20 minutes, stirring once or twice. Remove from the heat and let the rice stand for at least 15 minutes. Add the almonds to the rice and stir to combine. Transfer to a heated serving dish and serve immediately.

EL TEDDY'S · *TORTA DE TRES LECHES*

THIS RECIPE FOR a very traditional Mexican cake of three milks comes from El Teddy's Pastry Chef Judy Lyness. She splits the cake in half and fills it with mangoes before placing it in the milk bath. You may also serve the cake with freshly sliced strawberries and sweetened whipped cream, omitting the mangoes. The cake will then resemble a strawberry shortcake. Either way, the cake must be made the day before serving and refrigerated overnight.

MAKES ONE 9-INCH ROUND CAKE

The cake
1/2 cup sugar
4 eggs, separated
1/2 teaspoon vanilla
1 1/4 cups flour
1/2 teaspoon baking powder
3/8 cup milk
3 mangoes
juice of 1 lime

The milk bath
1/2 cup sweetened condensed milk
3/4 cup evaporated milk
1 1/2 teaspoons vanilla

To garnish and serve
1 cup heavy cream, whipped (for garnish)
1 to 2 pints fresh strawberries, hulled and sliced
  (for garnish)

To Make the Cake: Preheat the oven to 350 degrees. Grease a 9 x 2 inch round cake pan or an 8-inch square pan. In a large mixing bowl, beat 1/4 cup of the sugar with the egg yolks and vanilla using an electric mixer, until the mixture becomes lemony yellow and forms a ribbon. Set aside.

In a separate bowl, stir together the flour and baking powder. Alternate adding the flour and the milk to the egg-yolk mixture, stirring well after each addition. Set aside this batter.

Beat the egg whites in a large nonreactive bowl, using an electric mixer, until the egg whites get foamy. Add the remaining 1/4 cup sugar, and continue to beat the egg whites until they form soft peaks. Fold the egg whites gently into the batter. Pour the batter into the greased pan and bake for about 25 minutes, or until a skewer inserted into the center comes out clean. Remove from the oven. Cool for 5 minutes in the pan. Then invert onto a wire rack to cool completely.

Meanwhile, peel and dice the mangoes into 1/2-inch cubes and sprinkle them with lime juice. Split the cooled cake in half using a serrated knife. Arrange the mangoes evenly over the bottom half of the cake to within 1/4 inch of the

edge. Place the cake in a large plastic container with an airtight lid. Put the top half of the cake in place over the mangoes.

To Soak the Cake: Combine the sweetened condensed milk, the evaporated milk, and the vanilla in a small nonreactive bowl. Pour the mixture over the cake and let it soak in. Cover the container and store it in the refrigerator overnight. Baste the top of the cake with the milk mixture a few times and again just before removing from the pan to serve.

To Serve: Remove the cake from the milk bath and slice it. Serve the cake on individual dessert plates with whipped cream and strawberries.

MONTRACHET

Summer Menu

❧

MARINATED SQUID
& OCTOPUS SALAD
WITH SHERRY
VINAIGRETTE,
MANGO & RED
ONION

SWORDFISH WITH
ROSEMARY
POLENTA,
TOMATOES &
FRESH HERBS

PLUM *FINANCIER*
WITH PEACH
PURÉE

MARINATED SQUID & OCTOPUS SALAD WITH SHERRY VINAIGRETTE, MANGO & RED ONION

THIS DISH IS a unique and exciting blend of ingredients and is well worth the effort. The entire dish can be prepared in advance and assembled at the last moment. In fact, the preparation for this dish must begin at least three days in advance. The marinade must rest in the refrigerator for two days before you add the squid and octopus. So wait until the day before you serve the meal to purchase the squid and octopus.

SERVES SIX

The marinade
1/4 cup curry powder
1/2 cup olive oil
1/2 cup vegetable oil
1/2 sprig lemon grass, cut into 1/2-inch pieces

The seafood
3/4 pounds (about 1 1/2 cups) squid, cleaned, with heads removed
1 pound (about 2 cups) octopus, cleaned, with heads removed

Sherry vinaigrette
1/3 cup sherry vinegar
2 tablespoons shallots, finely chopped
1 cup olive oil
salt
freshly ground pepper

The salad
1/2 cup thinly sliced (1/8 inch thick) red onion rings
2 tablespoons olive oil
6 handfuls salad greens, washed and dried
1 mango, peeled and julienned

To Make the Marinade: Gently heat the curry powder in a heavy saucepan for 1 minute over medium heat. Remove from the heat and whisk in the olive oil and the vegetable oil. Transfer to a lidded jar and refrigerate for 2 days, stirring each day. Ladle

off the oil and reserve it. Measure I tablespoon of the curry oil solids and add it to the reserved oil. Discard the rest of the curry oil solids. Add the lemon grass and set aside this marinade.

To Marinate the Seafood: Cut the squid into 1/4-inch rounds. Cut the octopus bodies in half. Place this seafood in the curry oil marinade, cover, and refrigerate overnight.

To Make the Vinaigrette: In a medium-sized nonreactive bowl, combine the sherry vinegar with the shallots. Add the olive oil in a steady stream, whisking slowly to emulsify. Season with salt and pepper to taste. Set this dressing aside.

To Cook the Onions: Lightly rub the onion rings with 2 tablespoons of olive oil and grill them under the broiler, or sauté them quickly over high heat, until they begin to color. (They should not become soft.) Set aside.

To Cook the Seafood: Remove the marinated octopus and squid from the refrigerator. Strain it and remove the pieces of lemon grass. Heat a large cast-iron pan over high heat. Saute the octopus and squid until they are golden brown. Remove from the heat and season with salt and pepper.

To Serve: Toss the salad greens with enough Sherry Vinaigrette to lightly coat them. Add the mangoes and red onions and toss. Distribute the salad equally among 6 salad plates and top with equal portions of the squid and octopus.

MONTRACHET

SWORDFISH WITH ROSEMARY POLENTA, TOMATOES & FRESH HERBS

THE ROBUST FLAVORS of the tomatoes, preserved lemon, and olives are a delicious accompaniment to the delicate taste of the fish and polenta. The sauce may be prepared a few hours ahead and reheated before serving. However, you will first need to prepare the preserved lemon, which will take two weeks to marinate. See page 165 in the Basics and Techniques section for this step. For this dish, purchase center-cut pieces of swordfish.

SERVES SIX

Tomato sauce
2 tablespoons extra virgin olive oil
2 onions, thinly sliced
4 cloves garlic, thinly sliced
6 small ripe tomatoes, cored and diced
1/2 preserved lemon, julienned
12 Niçoise olives, pitted and cut in large pieces
8 fresh basil leaves, julienned
salt
freshly ground pepper

The polenta
1 quart chicken stock
3 tablespoons finely chopped fresh rosemary
1 tablespoon butter
2 1/4 cups cornmeal
2 tablespoons extra virgin olive oil

3 tablespoons heavy cream
salt
freshly ground pepper

The swordfish
6 1-inch-thick pieces swordfish (6 ounces each)
salt
freshly ground pepper
2 tablespoons olive oil

To Make the Tomato Sauce: Heat the olive oil in a large shallow pan over medium heat. Add the onions and garlic and cook them until they are translucent. Add the tomatoes, lemon, and olives. Cook over medium-low heat for 30 to 40 minutes, until the mixture is thick and bubbly. Add the basil and season with salt and pepper. Reduce the heat to low and cover the pan. Meanwhile, prepare the polenta.

To Make the Polenta: Place the chicken stock, rosemary, and butter in a large saucepan and bring the liquid to a boil over medium-high heat. Slowly add the cornmeal in a thin stream, whisking continuously while cooking, until the mixture is thick and bubbly. Boil for 1 or 2 minutes, stirring continuously. Reduce the heat to low and whisk in the olive oil and cream. Season with salt and pepper. Pour the mixture into a warm bowl, cover with plastic wrap, and set aside while you prepare the fish.

To Prepare the Fish: Season each side of the swordfish with salt and pepper. Heat the olive oil in a sauté pan over high heat. Add the fish and sauté on both sides until golden brown, about 4 minutes in all. (The fish should be slightly firm to the touch.) Remove from the heat and serve immediately.

To Serve: In the center of each warm dinner plate, place three large spoonfuls of the rosemary polenta. Place a piece of swordfish on top of polenta and surround the polenta with the tomato sauce.

<table>
</table>

MONTRACHET

PLUM *FINANCIER* WITH PEACH PURÉE

THE BATTER FOR these individual cakes must be chilled for at least one hour (and up to a full day) before baking. The cakes may be baked earlier in the day, stored in an airtight container, and reheated for five minutes in a 300-degree oven before serving.

Financiers are a classic French dessert that usually are baked in baking rings. If you don't have any baking rings, you can use small empty tuna cans or other six-ounce cans. Remove the top and bottom of each can and clean it thoroughly. Butter the inside of the rings, place them on a baking sheet lined with parchment paper, and fill them with batter. The ramekins recommended here are also a suitable substitute for baking rings.

SERVES SIX

The financier

1 cup unsalted butter
1 1/2 cups confectioners' sugar
2/3 cup flour
2/3 cup ground almonds
5 egg whites
3 plums

The peach purée

3 medium peaches, blanched and peeled, or 2 cups
    frozen peaches
2 tablespoons granulated sugar
1 teaspoon lemon juice

To Prepare the Financier: Cook the butter in a heavy saucepan over medium heat until it turns a nut-brown color. Meanwhile, sift the sugar and flour together into a large mixing bowl. Add the ground almonds and gently stir the ingredients together. Whisk in the egg whites. When the butter is ready, strain it through a sieve into the flour-and-egg mixture and whisk until the batter is smooth. Cover and refrigerate for at least 1 hour.

Preheat the oven to 400 degrees. Butter six 4-ounce ramekins and set them aside. Slice the plums into 1/8-inch slivers. Distribute the batter evenly among the ramekins. Arrange the plum slices in a circular pattern on top of the batter. Bake for 25 to 30 minutes, or until the cakes are golden brown. Remove the cakes from the ramekins immediately. Allow them to cool slightly on a wire rack.

To Prepare the Purée: Combine the peaches, sugar, and lemon juice in a blender or food processor and purée. Strain the mixture into a serving bowl and set it aside.

To Serve: Place each *financier* on a warm dessert plate. Surround the cake with peach purée and serve immediately.

TRIBECA GRILL

Summer Menu

FRESH FAVA
BEAN &
ASPARAGUS SOUP

SAUTÉ OF SOFT-
SHELL CRABS
WITH WILTED
SPINACH &
WARM SUMMER
TOMATO
VINAIGRETTE

BARBECUED
BREAST OF DUCK
WITH SWEET
CORN
SUCCOTASH

SPICED
SPOONBREAD

ORANGE CHIFFON
CAKE WITH
LEMON VERBENA
CUSTARD &
BERRY COMPOTE

FRESH FAVA BEAN & ASPARAGUS SOUP

BECAUSE THIS IS a summer menu, we recommend serving this soup chilled. However, Chef Pintabona says it can be served warm or cold. Either way, this soup can be made three days in advance and can be kept in the freezer for up to three months.

SERVES SIX

2 cups fresh fava beans, shelled
1 tablespoon olive oil
1 medium yellow onion, coarsely chopped
2 small leeks, well cleaned and coarsely chopped
2 celery stalks, coarsely chopped
5 cups chicken stock
2 pounds medium asparagus, trimmed and coarsely chopped (reserve the tips for garnish)
salt
freshly ground pepper
6 to 8 tablespoons crème fraîche or sour cream
asparagus tips, blanched, for garnish

To Prepare the Soup: Drop the fava beans in a pot of boiling water for about 2 minutes. Remove and immediately rinse the beans in cold water. Peel the beans. (Reserve the water to blanch the asparagus tips used for garnish.)

Heat the olive oil in a heavy saucepan over medium-high heat. Add the onions, leeks, and celery. Cover the pan and sweat the vegetables (see page 166) until they are soft but not browned. Add the chicken stock and bring the liquid to a boil. Boil for 5 minutes. Add the asparagus and fava beans. Bring the liquid to a boil again. Then lower the heat and simmer, covered, for 8 minutes. Remove from the heat, and allow the soup to cool slightly, uncovered. Purée the soup until smooth, using a blender or food processor. Season with salt and pepper to taste. Transfer the purée to a container, cover it, and refrigerate for at least 2 hours.

To Serve: Serve the soup with a dollop of crème fraîche or sour cream, and garnish with the blanched asparagus tips.

†WINE SUGGESTION

David Gordon, Wine Director at Tribeca Grill, has selected the following wines to be enjoyed with this meal: with the Fresh Fava Bean & Asparagus Soup an Iron Horse Brut, 1989; with the Sauté of Soft-Shell Crabs a Calera Viognier, 1993; with the Barbecued Breast of Duck a Signorello Pinot Noir Reserve, 1991; and with the Orange Chiffon Cake a Bonny Doon Vin de Glaciere Muscat, 1992.

TRIBECA GRILL — SAUTÉ OF SOFT-SHELL CRABS WITH WILTED SPINACH & WARM SUMMER TOMATO VINAIGRETTE

THE MIXTURE OF yellow and red tomatoes alongside the green spinach and crispy crabs presents a festive summer plate.

SERVES SIX

The tomato vinaigrette
3/4 cup extra virgin olive oil
2 tablespoons balsamic vinegar
juice of 1/2 lemon
1 pint combined yellow pear tomatoes and
    red cherry tomatoes, halved
1 small red beefsteak tomato, seeded and
    diced
1 small yellow beefsteak tomato, seeded and
    diced
1 shallot, minced
1/4 cup basil, julienned
salt
freshly ground pepper

Wilted spinach
1/4 cup olive oil
2 cloves garlic, minced
2 pounds fresh spinach, washed thoroughly
2 tablespoons water
pinch of salt
pinch of freshly ground pepper

The crabs
6 soft-shell crabs, eyes and gills removed, rinsed
    clean
1 cup milk
1 cup flour
6 tablespoons butter
6 tablespoons olive oil

Tribeca Grill
375 Greenwich Street, New York, NY 10013
212 · 941 · 3900

To Make the Vinaigrette: Whisk together the olive oil, balsamic vinegar, and lemon juice in a medium-sized nonreactive saucepan. Stir in the tomatoes, shallots, and basil. Season with salt and pepper to taste. Slowly heat the vinaigrette and keep it warm until ready to serve.

To Prepare the Spinach: Heat olive oil in a large sauté pan over medium-high heat. Add the garlic and sauté, stirring continuously so it doesn't burn. Add the spinach, water, salt, and pepper. Toss frequently and cook just until the spinach wilts. Remove from the heat and set aside.

To Prepare the Crabs: Soak the crabs in milk for 5 minutes. Dredge each crab in flour and shake off the excess. Heat the butter and olive oil in a large skillet over high heat until the oil is very hot. (If you are cooking the crabs in batches, divide the oil and butter accordingly.) Sauté the crabs for 6 to 8 minutes, until they are crisp and reddish-brown. (Turn them once halfway through the cooking time. Soft-shell crabs pop and splatter while they cook, so be careful not to stand too close.) Remove the crabs from the pan, blot them on paper towels, and keep them warm until you are ready to serve them.

To Serve: Distribute the wilted spinach evenly among 6 dinner plates. Place a crab beside each mound of spinach, and spoon the tomato vinaigrette around the spinach and the crab. Serve immediately.

TRIBECA GRILL — BARBECUED BREAST OF DUCK WITH SWEET CORN SUCCOTASH

THIS DISH OFFERS a wonderful blend of flavors and colors. The recipe incorporates the cooking technique "gastrique," which involves sweet-and-sour caramelization added to a stock. The sauce can be prepared as much as two weeks in advance and stored in the refrigerator. Reheat it slightly just before serving. If you cannot get large (drake) Muscovy duck breasts in your local market, check with the suppliers listed in the Sources Guide (page 169).

The key to the succotash recipe is to cook the vegetables just long enough to bring out their full flavors. Prepare the corn ahead of time by blanching it for three minutes in boiling water and removing the kernels with a sharp knife. Set the corn aside, covered, until you are ready to prepare the succotash.

SERVES SIX

The sauce
9 tablespoons sugar
1/2 cup water
1/2 cup lemon juice
3 tablespoons cider vinegar
1 teaspoon ground cumin
1 teaspoon mustard powder
12 cups rich stock (duck or chicken)

The duck
2 whole boneless drake (male) Muscovy duck
    breasts (about 1 3/4 pounds each)
freshly ground pepper

The corn succotash
2 tablespoons olive oil
4 cloves garlic, minced
1/2 teaspoon minced jalapeño
1 red bell pepper, diced
1 medium red onion, diced
1 bunch green onions, chopped
1/4 cup plus 2 tablespoons chopped cilantro or
    parsley
1 cup chicken stock
6 ears of corn, blanched, with kernels removed

To Make the Sauce: Combine the sugar, water, and lemon juice in a large, heavy saucepan. Bring the liquid to a boil over medium-high heat. Continue to cook the syrup for about 10 minutes, until it is a deep golden brown. Remove from the heat. Add the vinegar, cumin, and mustard powder, stirring to combine. Return the sauce to a low heat and simmer for 5 minutes. Add the rich stock and bring the liquid to a boil. Continue cooking for 45 to 60 minutes, until the sauce is shiny and syrupy and has reduced to about 1 1/2 cups. Remove from the heat and set it aside.

To Barbecue the Duck: Prepare the grill. Cut the thick layer of fat from the duck. Place the duck breasts on a large plate or baking sheet and dust them lightly with freshly ground pepper. Grill the duck for about 8 minutes. (Halfway through the grilling time, turn the duck over.) Remove from the grill. Let the duck rest for 5 minutes. Then slice it. Begin the succotash while the duck is grilling.

To Prepare the Succotash: Heat the olive oil in a large skillet over low heat. Stir in the garlic and jalapeño. Increase the heat to medium-high and add the red bell pepper, onions, green onions, and cilantro or parsley. Toss to combine. Then add the chicken stock, lower the heat, and simmer for 5 minutes. Add the corn, remove from the heat, and adjust the seasoning.

To Serve: Place two large spoonfuls of succotash on each warm dinner plate. Serve the duck slices on top of the succotash. Spoon a little sauce over the duck and serve immediately.

SPICED SPOONBREAD

THE JALAPEÑO PROVIDES a flavor twist in this classic corn bread recipe. The sugar and honey soften the hot pepper flavor and give this spoonbread a crisp textured crust. Serve the bread warm. It should take about the same amount of time to bake as it takes to grill the Barbecued Breast of Duck. You can also make the spoonbread earlier in the day and reheat it in a 300-degree oven for about 10 minutes before you serve it.

SERVES SIX

1/2 cup cornmeal
2/3 cup flour
1/2 teaspoon baking powder
4 tablespoons butter, softened to room
    temperature
6 tablespoons sugar
2 eggs
1/3 cup milk
2 tablespoons honey
1 teaspoon finely chopped jalapeño

Preheat the oven to 350 degrees. Butter an 8-inch square baking pan. Mix together the cornmeal, flour, and baking powder in a large bowl. Set aside. Cream together the butter and sugar in the bowl of an electric mixer until combined. Add the eggs, one at a time, and continue to beat the mixture. Gradually add the milk.

Stir the wet ingredients into the dry ingredients, using a fork, mixing just until combined. Add the honey and the jalapeño and combine with a few quick strokes. Pour the batter into the prepared pan and bake for 20 minutes, or until a toothpick inserted in the center comes out clean. Serve immediately.

ORANGE CHIFFON CAKE WITH LEMON VERBENA CUSTARD & BERRY COMPOTE

THESE ORANGE CHIFFON cakes are as light as a feather. They are complemented nicely by the subtly flavored lemon verbena custard. If you cannot find lemon verbena, which is a summer herb, you can substitute mint, although the flavor will be stronger. The berry compote takes ten days to complete. Choose any kind of berries except blueberries. Note that you will need only two cups of fruit at first. Then, after four days, you will add fruit each day for six days. Purchase the fruit accordingly. The

compote will keep in the refrigerator for up to five months. The lemon verbena custard can be made one day in advance. You can also make the cakes earlier in the day and store them in an airtight container. The final presentation is colorful, elegant, and delicious.

SERVES SIX

The compote
8 cups fresh mixed berries, washed and hulled
    (See note above regarding berries.)
5 cups sugar

The custard
1 cup milk
1/4 cup coarsely chopped lemon verbena
4 egg yolks
1 tablespoon plus 1 teaspoon cornstarch
4 tablespoons sugar

The cake
3 tablespoons superfine sugar
1/2 cup cake flour
3/4 teaspoon baking powder
1/4 teaspoon salt
1 tablespoon peanut oil
1 egg yolk
2 tablespoons freshly squeezed orange juice
zest of 1 orange
1/2 teaspoon vanilla extract
2 egg whites
1/4 teaspoon cream of tartar
confectioners' sugar
6 sprigs fresh mint for garnish

To Make the Compote: Combine 2 cups of berries and 2 cups of sugar in a clean 2-liter mason jar and cover the opening with cheesecloth, securing it with a rubber band. Place the jar in the refrigerator and stir the compote daily, taking care not to crush the berries.

After 4 days, mix together 1 cup of berries and 1/2 cup of sugar and add this mixture to the mason jar of fruit. Stir gently. Repeat each day for 5 more days. Keep the jar covered loosely with cheesecloth and store it in the refrigerator.

To Make the Custard: Place 3/4 cup milk in a nonreactive saucepan with the lemon verbena. Bring the milk to a boil. Meanwhile, combine the egg yolks, cornstarch, remaining 1/4 cup milk, and the sugar in a small nonreactive bowl. Beat the mixture until the ingredients are well combined. Slowly pour the milk into the egg-yolk mixture, whisking constantly. Return the mixture to the saucepan. Cook the custard over low heat, stirring constantly with

a wooden spoon, until the custard thickens. Remove the pan from the heat and pass the mixture through a fine sieve into a mixing bowl that is sitting in an ice bath. When cool transfer the custard to a chilled ceramic bowl and cover it with plastic wrap. Chill until ready to serve.

To Make the Cake: Preheat the oven to 325 degrees. Butter and flour a 6-cup muffin tin. Reserve 1 teaspoon of the sugar, and sift together the remaining sugar with the flour, baking powder, and salt in a large nonreactive bowl. Set aside. In a separate bowl, whisk together the oil, egg yolk, orange juice, zest, and vanilla extract. Make a well in the dry ingredients and add the combined wet ingredients. Fold gently using a wire whisk.

Beat the egg whites in a small nonreactive bowl until they are frothy. Add the cream of tartar and continue beating until the egg whites hold soft peaks. Add the reserved 1 teaspoon of sugar and continue beating the egg whites until they are stiff. Fold the egg-white mixture into the egg-yolk mixture. Spoon the batter into the prepared muffin tins. Bake for 20 minutes or until the tops are golden brown. Remove from the oven and cool on a wire rack for 5 minutes. Then remove the cakes from the muffin tin and let them cool completely.

To Serve: Place each cake on an individual dessert plate. Top it with a dollop of lemon verbena custard. Spoon berry compote around the cake and sprinkle confectioners' sugar through a sieve over the entire dessert. Garnish each plate with a sprig of mint.

TWO ELEVEN RESTAURANT

Summer Menu

COLD CURRIED
CARROT SOUP
WITH CILANTRO

BROILED SALMON
WITH BRAISED
ESCAROLE &
FRIED LEEK
GARNISH

ORZO WITH
LEMON THYME
ZUCCHINI BROTH

CHOCOLATE
CHUNK
HAZELNUT CAKE
WITH RASPBERRY
SAUCE &
WHIPPED CREAM

COLD CURRIED CARROT SOUP WITH CILANTRO

BECAUSE THIS SOUP is served cold, it can be made well in advance. You can keep it in the refrigerator for up to four days or in the freezer for up to four months. This recipe serves eight as a first course or four as a light main course, with a hearty bread and salad.

SERVES EIGHT

4 tablespoons extra virgin olive oil
2 medium yellow onions, coarsely chopped
3 medium celery stalks, coarsely chopped
10 medium carrots, coarsely chopped
2 jalapeños, seeded and coarsely chopped
1 2-inch piece ginger root, peeled and coarsely chopped
1/4 cup fresh cilantro, chopped
1 teaspoon cinnamon
1 teaspoon curry powder
1 teaspoon ground cumin
8 cups water
salt
freshly ground pepper
8 sprigs fresh cilantro for garnish

Place the olive oil, onions, celery, carrots, jalapeños, ginger root, and chopped cilantro in a heavy stockpot and stir to coat all of the vegetables. Cover the pot and cook over medium heat for 25 minutes, until the vegetables are soft. Add the cinnamon, curry powder, and cumin and stir. Cook for a few minutes with the cover off. Then add the water and bring the liquid to a boil. Lower the heat and simmer the soup, uncovered, for 30 minutes. Remove from the heat and allow the soup to cool slightly. Then purée it in batches in a food processor or blender until it is completely smooth. Season with salt and pepper to taste. Chill the soup before serving. Garnish with sprigs of fresh cilantro.

†WINE SUGGESTION

Tom Oliva, General Manager at Two Eleven, recommends the following wines to be served with this menu: With the Cold Curried Carrot Soup and with the Broiled Salmon a Guenoc Estate Bottled 1993 Chardonnay from Guenoc Valley, California; with the Chocolate Chunk Hazelnut Cake a 1990 Peter Lehmann Sauternes.

TWO ELEVEN RESTAURANT

BROILED SALMON WITH BRAISED ESCAROLE & FRIED LEEK GARNISH

THIS DISH IS quick to prepare. Serve it with the Orzo with Lemon Thyme Zucchini Broth, which you can prepare ahead of time.

SERVES EIGHT

The leek garnish
2 leeks, tops removed
vegetable oil

The escarole
4 tablespoons olive oil
2 shallots, finely chopped
3 cloves garlic, finely chopped
6 cups chopped escarole (1 to 2 bunches)
1/4 cup water

The salmon
1 tablespoon each: fresh thyme, tarragon, and
   parsley, finely chopped
salt
freshly ground pepper
8 7-ounce pieces salmon fillet, skinned
4 tablespoons olive oil

To Prepare the Leeks: Quarter the leeks lengthwise. Clean them thoroughly, pat them dry, and julienne them. Heat a cast-iron skillet over medium-high heat and add vegetable oil to a depth of about 1/2 inch. Heat the oil until it is hot but not smoking. Fry the leeks in the oil in small batches until they are golden brown. Lift them from the pan and place them on paper towels to drain. Set them aside.

To Braise the Escarole: Heat the olive oil in a heavy saucepan over medium-high heat. Add the shallots and garlic and cook for 5 minutes, until they are soft but not browned. Add the escarole and water. Braise the escarole for 15 minutes, stirring often. Meanwhile, prepare the salmon.

To Prepare the Salmon: Mix the chopped fresh herbs together in a small dish and stir in the salt and pepper. Sprinkle this mixture over the salmon fillets. Spread about 3 tablespoons of olive oil on a broiler pan. Transfer the salmon to the broiler pan and drizzle the remaining 1 tablespoon of olive oil over them. Broil the fish for 6 to 8 minutes, or until it flakes easily.

To Serve: Make a bed of escarole on each of 6 warm dinner plates. Place a salmon fillet on top of the escarole and garnish with the fried leeks.

TWO ELEVEN RESTAURANT

ORZO WITH LEMON THYME ZUCCHINI BROTH

THIS ENTIRE COLORFUL dish can be prepared in advance. You can keep the broth at room temperature for several hours or in the refrigerator for up to four days. Whisk the ingredients together as you reheat the broth.

SERVES EIGHT

The broth

4 small to medium-sized zucchini, trimmed
1/2 cup olive oil
1 clove garlic, finely chopped
1 tablespoon finely chopped lemon thyme
salt
freshly ground pepper

The orzo

salt
1/2 pound orzo
4 tablespoons olive oil

2 cloves garlic, finely chopped
1 green bell pepper, finely chopped
1 red bell pepper, finely chopped
1 yellow bell pepper, finely chopped
1 small red onion, finely chopped
salt
freshly ground pepper

To Prepare the Broth: Press the zucchini using a juicer. (Or cut it into large cubes and liquefy in a blender or food processor. Then pass the liquid through a fine sieve.) Measure out 2 cups of juice and set aside.

Heat 1/4 cup of the olive oil and garlic in a large, covered saucepan at a medium temperature until the garlic is soft but not browned. Stir in the lemon thyme. Add the zucchini juice, whisk, and heat until the liquid comes to a boil. Remove from the heat and pour the liquid into a blender or food processor. While the blender is running, slowly add the remaining 1/4 cup olive oil and blend until fully combined. Set the broth aside.

To Prepare the Orzo: Fill a large pot with water and add a pinch of salt. Bring the water to a boil and add the orzo. Cook until the pasta is al dente.

Meanwhile, heat 2 tablespoons of the olive oil with the garlic in a heavy saucepan, covered, over medium-high heat until the garlic is soft but not browned. Add the bell peppers and onions and cover again. Continue cooking for 10 to 15 minutes, until the vegetables are soft.

Drain the orzo and rinse it under cool water. Transfer it to a serving bowl, add the remaining 2 tablespoons of olive oil, and toss. Add the cooked bell pepper mixture to the orzo and mix well. Season with salt and pepper to taste. Serve the orzo at room temperature, surrounding the Braised Escarole. Pour the warm zucchini broth around the orzo and let it seep into the pasta.

TWO ELEVEN RESTAURANT

CHOCOLATE CHUNK HAZELNUT CAKE WITH RASPBERRY SAUCE & WHIPPED CREAM

THERE IS NOTHING difficult about preparing this cake, and guests will be suitably impressed with the professional presentation and rich taste. Make the raspberry sauce while the cake is in the oven.

MAKES ONE 10-INCH CAKE

The cake
1 1/2 cups chopped semisweet chocolate
   or 1 1/2 cups semisweet chocolate chips
1 cup finely ground hazelnuts
2 tablespoons plain bread crumbs
1/2 teaspoon baking powder
1 cup butter, softened to room
   temperature
1 cup sugar
7 eggs, separated
2 tablespoons Amaretto

Raspberry sauce
1 pint fresh raspberries, washed, or 2 cups frozen
   raspberries, thawed
2 tablespoons sugar
1 tablespoon raspberry liqueur

Garnish
confectioners' sugar
1/2 pint heavy cream

To Make the Cake: Preheat the oven to 350 degrees. Butter a 10-inch springform pan. Line the bottom of the pan with waxed paper. Then butter the lining and flour the entire pan and lining.

Combine the chocolate, hazelnuts, bread crumbs, and baking powder in a medium-sized bowl. Stir to mix thoroughly. Set aside.

Cream the butter in a large mixing bowl using an electric mixer. Add the sugar and blend until creamy. Add the egg yolks, one at a time, and blend thoroughly. Add the Amaretto and blend. Stir the chocolate mixture into the butter mixture. Set aside this batter.

In a separate bowl, beat the egg whites until soft peaks form. Gently stir one-fourth of the egg whites into the batter. Gently fold the remaining egg whites into the batter until thoroughly combined. Pour the batter into the prepared pan and bake the cake on the lowest shelf of the oven for 50 to 60 minutes, or until a toothpick inserted into the center comes out clean. Remove from the oven and place on a wire rack to cool. (The cake will immediately shrink away from the sides of the pan and form wrinkles on the top. It will also have a wonderful nut brown color.) Invert the cake and take it out of the pan. Using a sharp knife, loosen the edges of the waxed paper and remove it. Reinvert the cake onto a serving dish. Set aside.

To Make the Raspberry Sauce: Place the raspberries in a blender or food processor with the sugar and the liqueur, and process until smooth. Pass the sauce through a sieve to remove most of the seeds. Chill the sauce.

To Serve: Just before serving, dust the cake with confectioners' sugar, sprinkled through a fine sieve. Whip the cream in a small nonreactive bowl, using an electric mixer. Slice the cake thinly using a sharp knife. Swirl some of the chilled raspberry sauce on each dessert plate. Place a slice of cake in the center of the plate, and top it with a dollop of whipped cream. Serve immediately.

FALL

THE CLEAVER COMPANY

Fall Menu

❧

A Cocktail Party

CHEESE STRAWS

MOROCCAN
CHICKEN WRAPPED
IN PHYLLO WITH A
ROASTED PEPPER
DIPPING SAUCE

CUCUMBER STARS
WITH SMOKED
SALMON CREAM

ENDIVE WITH
ROQUEFORT &
WALNUTS

OYSTERS IN
CHAMPAGNE SAUCE

BLUE POTATOES
WITH CRÈME
FRAÎCHE & CAVIAR

RATATOUILLE
TARTLETS

TEA-SMOKED
SHRIMP WRAPPED
IN SPINACH

CHEESE STRAWS

KEEP A BATCH of dough for these cheese straws on hand for company during the holiday season. You can freeze the dough or the unbaked straws in an airtight container for up to one month. The recipe calls for one pound of Gruyère cheese, but the straws are also tasty if you substitute Cheddar for the Gruyère or use half of each. Make sure you roll out the dough to an even thickness so the cheese straws will bake evenly.

MAKES ABOUT 72 STRAWS

1 pound Gruyère
   cheese, grated
1 cup butter, softened
   to room
   temperature
2 eggs
2 1/2 cups flour
1/2 teaspoon salt
1/2 teaspoon cayenne pepper
2 bunches green onions, finely chopped
6 tablespoons toasted sesame seeds

Beat the cheese and the butter together in a food processor or using an electric mixer. Add the eggs, one at a time, beating thoroughly. Add the flour, salt, and cayenne, and mix until combined. Turn the dough onto a lightly floured board, work the green onions into the dough by hand, and knead until smooth. Pat the dough into 3 thick rectangles, wrap them in waxed paper or plastic wrap, and refrigerate 1 hour or freeze at this point.

Preheat the oven to 375 degrees. Roll out one of the chilled rectangles on a lightly floured board into a rectangle about 12 x 5 inches with a thickness of about 1/8 inch. Sprinkle 2 tablespoons of sesame seeds over the rolled-out dough and gently push the seeds into the dough. Trim the edges of the dough so they are straight. Reserve the trimmings to rework later. Cut the dough into 5-inch-long strips, about 1/2-inch wide. Twist each strip twice and place the strip on a baking sheet. Repeat until all of the dough is used. Bake the straws for about 10 minutes (slightly longer if the dough is frozen), until they are golden brown. Place them on a wire rack to cool.

✝WINE SUGGESTION

The Cleaver Company relies on inspired wine advice from New York's Rosenthal Wine Merchant when planning special events. For the Fall Cocktail Party Rosenthal recommends a Mâcon La Roche-Vineuse, Domaine du Vieux Saint-Sorlin and a Champagne Cattier Brut ler Cru, non-vintage.

Moroccan Chicken Wrapped in Phyllo with a Roasted Pepper Dipping Sauce

THIS IS A variation of the traditional Moroccan dish, bisteeya, in which chicken, eggs, and almonds are layered, wrapped in phyllo, and baked in a large round loaf. In this recipe the ingredients are combined and wrapped into bite-size servings. These can be prepared in advance and stored (with each layer separated by parchment or waxed paper) in an airtight container in the freezer for up to two months before baking. (If you prefer to make fewer hors d'oeuvres, you can cut the recipe in half. Use half of a chicken or one whole chicken breast, and simmer it for 30 minutes.) The roasted pepper sauce can be prepared up to three days in advance.

MAKES ABOUT 84 HORS D'OEUVRES

The chicken filling

2 tablespoons chopped garlic
1/2 cup chopped fresh cilantro or flat-leaf
   parsley
1 3 1/2-pound chicken, halved
1 cup butter
6 cups water
1 large onion, coarsely chopped
1 cinnamon stick
pinch of saffron
1/2 teaspoon turmeric
1 teaspoon fresh ginger, grated

1 teaspoon freshly ground pepper
1/4 cup lemon juice
10 eggs, lightly beaten

The nuts
3/4 pound blanched almonds
1/4 cup vegetable oil
1/3 cup confectioners' sugar
1/2 teaspoon ground cinnamon

The assembly
1 package phyllo dough
1/2 cup butter, melted

Roasted Pepper Dipping Sauce
3 red bell peppers, roasted (see page 166)
3 cloves garlic
1/2 cup olive oil
juice of 1 lemon
dash of Tabasco sauce
pinch of salt
pinch of freshly ground pepper

To Make the Filling: Combine the garlic with the cilantro or parsley in a food processor and blend until smooth. Spread this mixture on the chicken halves and place them in a heavy saucepan over medium heat. Add the butter, water, onions, cinnamon stick, saffron, turmeric, ginger, salt, and pepper. Bring the liquid to a boil, cover, and simmer for 1 hour.

Remove the chicken and let it cool. Meanwhile, increase the heat under the saucepan and continue cooking, reducing the liquid to 3 cups. Add the lemon juice and lower the heat to a simmer. Add the eggs and cook for 10 minutes, stirring constantly while the eggs curdle. Remove from the heat. Strain the mixture and discard the liquid and cinnamon stick. Set aside this egg mixture.

Preheat the oven to 300 degrees. Place the almonds in a small bowl, add the oil, and toss. Spread the almonds on a baking sheet and roast them about 10 minutes, until they are golden brown. Remove from the oven and let them cool completely. Grind them in a food processor, using a pulse action until they have the consistency of pebbly sand. Add the confectioners' sugar and ground cinnamon and toss. Combine this with the egg mixture. Set aside.

Skin the chicken, and discard the skin. Pull the meat from the bones and chop it fine. Combine the chicken with the egg-and-almond mixture. Set aside this filling.

To Assemble the Pastries: Unroll the phyllo dough and cover it with a damp kitchen towel to keep it moist. Remove one sheet and place it on a flat surfce with the longest edge toward you. Brush it lightly with melted butter. Cover it with a second sheet and brush that one with melted butter. With a sharp knife, cut these sheets lengthwise into 8 strips. Place 1 teaspoon of filling near one end of each strip. Fold the end of the strip diagonally over the filling and continue to fold up the strip to form a triangle. Brush the top of each triangle with melted butter. Continue making triangles until you have used all of the filling.

Preheat the oven to 350 degrees. Place the prepared triangles on baking sheets and bake them for 15 to 20 minutes, until lightly browned. Remove them from the oven. Serve them hot or at room temperature with the dipping sauce.

To Prepare the Dipping Sauce: Purée the peppers and garlic in a food processor. While the processor is running, pour the olive oil into the purée in a steady stream. Add the lemon juice, Tabasco sauce, salt, and pepper. Transfer the sauce to a serving bowl, cover it, and store it in the refrigerator until ready to serve.

CUCUMBER STARS WITH SMOKED SALMON CREAM

THE CLEAVER COMPANY

THESE HORS D'OEUVRES are visually pleasing as well as tasty. Choose large, thick cucumbers that will give you big enough slices to cut with a small cookie cutter.

MAKES 48 HORS D'OEUVRES

2 to 3 large cucumbers
1/4 pound smoked salmon
1/2 pound cream cheese
1/2 tablespoon lemon juice
1/2 teaspoon freshly ground pepper
salmon roe for garnish
sprigs of dill for garnish

Cut the cucumbers into 1/2-inch-thick slices. Using a star-shaped cookie cutter small enough to fit inside the cucumber rounds, cut each slice into a star shape. Scoop out a well in each cucumber star, using a melon baller or small spoon. (Be careful not to break through the bottom of the cucumber slice.) Place the slices upside-down on paper towels to drain. Meanwhile, prepare the salmon cream.

Combine the smoked salmon, cream cheese, lemon juice, and pepper in a food processor. Process until smooth. Adjust the seasoning. Fit a pastry bag with a 1/2-inch round tip. Spoon the salmon cream into the bag. Fill the scooped-out cucumber slices with salmon cream, and garnish each one with salmon roe and a tiny sprig of dill.

THE CLEAVER COMPANY

ENDIVE WITH ROQUEFORT & WALNUTS

THESE HORS D'OEUVRES offer a simple and pleasing combination of ingredients. They are quick and easy to prepare, too. You may prepare the cheese mixture one day in advance, but fill the endive leaves an hour or so before you serve them. Use only the large outer leaves of the endive; reserve the small inner leaves for a salad.

MAKES ABOUT 24 HORS D'OEUVRES

1/2 cup walnuts
1/2 cup Roquefort cheese
1/2 cup sour cream
4 endives
several sprigs flat-leaf parsley, or edible flowers
    (such as nasturtium), julienned, for garnish

Preheat the oven to 400 degrees. Place the walnuts on a baking sheet and toast them for 5 minutes, or until they are lightly browned. Remove them from the oven and allow the walnuts to cool. Then coarsely chop them. In a medium-sized bowl, combine the walnuts with the Roquefort cheese and sour cream. Mix until the cheese is crumbly but not completely smooth.

Separate the endive leaves. Place about 1 teaspoon of the cheese mixture at the base of each leaf. Arrange the leaves on a serving tray. Garnish each leaf with parsley or the julienned edible flowers.

THE CLEAVER COMPANY

OYSTERS IN CHAMPAGNE SAUCE

THESE OYSTERS ARE also appropriate as a first course for a dinner party. When you purchase the oysters, ask the fishmonger to open them and reserve the liquid. Keep half of the shells for serving and discard the rest. You can prepare the oysters in advance and then broil them just before serving.

MAKES 36 OYSTERS

3 cups Champagne
liquid from the oysters
36 large oysters
14 tablespoons butter
6 shallots, minced
2 heads Boston lettuce or spinach
juice of 1 lemon
4 egg yolks
36 oyster shells

Combine 2 cups of the Champagne with the oyster liquid and the oysters in a saucepan. Heat gently until the oysters are warm and the edges are just beginning to curl. Strain the oysters and set them aside. Reserve the poaching liquid.

Heat 4 tablespoons of butter in a heavy-bottomed saucepan over medium heat. Add the shallots and cook them until they are soft and transparent. Add the poaching liquid and the remaining 1 cup of Champagne. Increase the heat to high and reduce the liquid to about 4 tablespoons of syrup. (Watch it carefully to make sure it doesn't burn.) Meanwhile, prepare the lettuce or spinach.

The
TRIBECA

CHOOKBOOK

32 · BUTTERCHEESE EGGS · 182

Bring water to a boil in a large saucepan. Drop the lettuce or spinach leaves in the water for about 30 seconds. Remove and immediately run under cold water. Wrap each oyster in a separate leaf, placing the rib of the leaf on top of the oyster and tucking the edges underneath. Set these aside.

When the sauce has reduced, add the lemon juice and remove the pan from the heat. Let the sauce cool slightly. Then add the egg yolks, whisking well. Return the pan to low heat and add the remaining butter, I tablespoon at a time, whisking until the sauce is the consistency of mayonnaise. Remove from the heat and adjust the seasoning.

To Serve: Preheat the broiler. Place a wrapped oyster in each shell. Spoon 2 teaspoons of sauce over each one. Arrange the oyster shells on a baking sheet and place under the broiler for 3 minutes, until the sauce is lightly browned. Remove from the broiler and serve immediately.

THE CLEAVER COMPANY BLUE POTATOES WITH CRÈME FRAÎCHE & CAVIAR

YOU CAN VARY this classic hors d'oeuvre recipe according to your budget and the availability of ingredients. You can use new red potatoes instead of blue potatoes, and salmon roe instead of sevruga caviar. The potatoes may be prepared ahead of time and held at room temperature. Fill and garnish just before serving.

MAKES 48 HORS D'OEUVRES

24 blue potatoes, I–2 inches in diameter
salt
freshly ground pepper
2 tablespoons olive oil
1/2 cup crème fraîche or sour cream
2 ounces sevruga caviar
sprigs of dill or chives for garnish

Preheat the oven to 350 degrees. Scrub the potatoes and cut each one in half. Remove a small slice from the bottom of each potato half so it will sit flat. With a melon baller or small spoon, scoop out a well from each potato half. Arrange the potatoes on a baking sheet. Sprinkle them with salt, pepper, and olive oil. Bake them for 15 minutes, or until they can be pierced easily with a sharp knife. Remove from the oven and let them cool.

To serve: Fill each potato with crème fraîche or sour cream and a little caviar. Garnish each one with a sprig of dill or chives. Serve immediately.

THE CLEAVER COMPANY

RATATOUILLE TARTLETS

BOTH THE SHELLS and the filling for these colorful tartlets can be prepared ahead of time. The prebaked shells may be stored in an airtight container until ready to serve. Bake the tartlets in one- to two-inch fluted tartlet molds, preferably tin ones.

MAKES ABOUT 48 TARTLETS

The shells
1 cup unsalted butter
2 1/2 cups flour
1/2 teaspoon salt
1/4 to 1/2 cup water

The ratatouille filling
3 tablespoons olive oil
1 small red onion, diced small
1 small red bell pepper, diced small
1 small zucchini, diced small
1 small yellow squash, diced small
2 tomatoes—peeled, seeded, and diced small
1/2 teaspoon chopped fresh thyme
1/2 teaspoon chopped fresh rosemary
1/4 teaspoon salt
1/2 teaspoon freshly ground pepper

1/2 cup chopped Italian parsley, for garnish

To Make the Shells: Combine the butter, flour and salt in a food processor and blend well, using a pulse action. Transfer the dough to a mixing bowl. Add the water, a little at a time, and toss gently with your fingers until it can be packed into a ball. Flatten the dough ball, wrap it in plastic, and refrigerate it for at least 1 hour or until ready to bake. (You may wish to make the ratatouille filling meanwhile.)

Preheat the oven to 400 degrees. Work half of the dough at a time, keeping the second half chilled. Roll the dough on a lightly floured board to 1/8-inch thickness. Using a cookie cutter that is slightly larger than the tartlet molds, cut out rounds of dough and press them into the tartlet molds, trimming any excess on the edges. Prick the dough all over with a fork. Bake for 12 minutes, until the shells just begin to brown. (Check halfway through baking. If the shells are rising out of the molds, prick them again or press them

back down.) Remove from the oven and place on a wire rack to cool. Remove the shells from the molds and bake the second batch in the same manner.

To Make the Filling: Heat the olive oil in a sauté pan over medium-high heat. Add the onions and bell peppers and sauté for 3 minutes. Add the zucchini and yellow squash and continue cooking for another 3 minutes, or until the vegetables are slightly soft. Add the tomatoes, thyme, rosemary, salt, and pepper. Toss to combine and cook for 2 more minutes. Remove from the heat and let the ratatouille cool.

To Serve: Fill each shell with ratatouille filling and garnish with parsley.

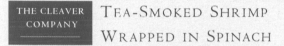

THE CLEAVER COMPANY TEA-SMOKED SHRIMP WRAPPED IN SPINACH

THIS RECIPE USES a traditional Chinese smoking technique, which is not difficult to do. Use a wok or cast-iron pan with a lid. Smoke the shrimp in batches. The shrimp may be smoked up to one week in advance and stored covered in the refrigerator. This will greatly enhance their flavor. You may wrap them several hours before serving.

MAKES ABOUT 60 HORS D'OEUVRES

The shrimp
1/2 cup flour
1/2 cup brown sugar
1/2 cup lapsang-souchong tea leaves
2 pounds large shrimp (about 60), peeled and deveined
1/2 cup sesame oil

The wrapping
1/2 pound fresh spinach, washed thoroughly
2 bunches whole chives
soy sauce for dipping

To Smoke the Shrimp: Line the wok completely with aluminum foil, allowing it to come up the sides so there will be enough foil to form a tent over the shrimp. Combine the flour, brown sugar, and tea leaves in the wok on the aluminum foil lining. Place a rack over this mixture and arrange the shrimp on the rack, preferably in a single layer. Fold the foil edges together and seal them so the shrimp are completely enclosed. Cover the wok with its lid. Place the wok on a high heat. From the time that the ingredients begin to smoke, cook the shrimp for 5 minutes. Turn off the heat and allow the wok to stand for an additional 10 minutes. Slowly remove the lid and gently unseal the aluminum foil. Remove the shrimp and brush them lightly with the sesame oil.

To Wrap the Shrimp: Blanch the spinach leaves for 30 seconds in boiling water. Remove them immediately and rinse them in cold water. Spread the spinach leaves on towels to dry. Meanwhile, blanch the chives briefly.

Cut the spines from the spinach leaves, and cut each leaf into 1-inch strips. Wrap a spinach strip around the middle of each shrimp, allowing the pink ends of the shrimp to show. Tie it with a chive.

To Serve: Arrange the shrimp on a platter and serve them with soy sauce.

DUANE PARK CAFE

Fall Menu

❦

WARM GOATS'
MILK CHEESE IN
PHYLLO WITH
ROASTED BEETS

ROASTED
CHICKEN WITH
OREGANO
BRUSCHETTA
STUFFING

OVEN-DRIED
TOMATOES &
WHIPPED WHITE
BEANS

QUINCE FRITTERS
WITH CIDER
CARAMEL &
WALNUT BRITTLE
ICE CREAM

WARM GOATS' MILK CHEESE IN PHYLLO WITH ROASTED BEETS

THIS FIRST COURSE makes an exciting and elegant presentation. It is full of flavor and is very simple to make, despite the lengthy instructions. The beets may be prepared one day in advance and stored, covered, in the refrigerator. The cheese can be wrapped in the phyllo and kept in the refrigerator a few hours before serving. You can use walnuts in these pastries, but hazelnuts are preferable. Substitute any similar lettuce for the oak leaf lettuce.

SERVES EIGHT

The beets
4 medium-sized beets, washed and with tops
    removed
vegetable oil

The phyllo pastries
1/4 cup finely chopped hazelnuts
1/4 cup finely chopped fresh sage

8 sheets phyllo dough
1/2 cup butter, melted
salt
freshly ground pepper
8-ounce log of firm goats' milk cheese, sliced into
    8 rounds

The salad
juice of 1 lemon
1/4 cup olive oil
8 small handfuls oak leaf lettuce, washed and
    dried

To Prepare the Beets: Preheat the oven to 375 degrees. Lightly rub the beets with vegetable oil and place them on a baking sheet. Roast the beets for 20 to 30 minutes, until they pierce easily with a sharp knife. Remove from the oven and allow to cool slightly. Peel the beets and set them aside.

To Prepare the Pastries: Combine the nuts and sage in a bowl and set aside. Place one sheet of phyllo on a flat surface. (Cover the remaining sheets with a damp dish towel to prevent them from drying out.) Brush the phyllo dough with melted butter

†WINE SUGGESTION

General Manager Alfred A. Chiodo recommends serving a selection of American wines with this menu. A Meridian Chardonnay, 1992, from Santa Barbara County to accompany the Warm Goats' Cheese in Phyllo; a Calera Pinot Noir, 1991, from the Central Coast to accompany the Roasted Chicken; and a Joseph Phelps Late Harvest Riesling, 1990, to accompany the Quince Fritters.

and sprinkle with one-eighth of the nut mixture on top. Season lightly with salt and pepper. Place a second sheet of phyllo on top and repeat this method until you have used four sheets. (End with the phyllo on top.)

Using kitchen scissors, carefully cut through the layered phyllo across the width to form 4 short strips. At the end of each strip, place a piece of cheese at one corner. Roll the cheese in the phyllo strip, keeping it at one end. Brush the seam with melted butter. Stand the roll up, cheese-end-down, on a baking sheet. Repeat this procedure with the remaining sheets of phyllo dough and cheese until you have 8 rolls. Refrigerate the rolls while you prepare the salad.

To Make the Salad Dressing: Combine the lemon juice with the olive oil and season with salt and pepper.

To Assemble the Dish: Slice the beets about 1/8-inch thick. Dip the slices into the salad dressing and arrange them evenly and slightly overlapping on 8 salad plates. Set aside.

Preheat the oven to 400 degrees. Bake the phyllo rolls on the lowest shelf of the oven for 8 to 10 minutes, or until the phyllo is golden brown and the cheese is warm. Meanwhile, lightly toss the lettuce with the remaining dressing, and divide it equally among the 8 salad plates, mounding it on top of the beets to form a bed for the phyllo rolls. Set aside. Remove the phyllo rolls from oven. Lift the rolls carefully from the pan using a metal spatula. Place each roll on a mound of lettuce on the salad plate. Serve immediately.

ROASTED CHICKEN WITH OREGANO BRUSCHETTA STUFFING

THE STUFFING CAN be prepared and baked one day in advance and then stored, covered, in the refrigerator. Bring it to room temperature and then reheat the casserole in a 300-degree oven for 10 minutes. Place it in the oven as you remove the roasted chickens; that way, the timing should be perfect.

SERVES EIGHT

The stuffing

2 medium-sized loaves of Italian- or French-style bread
2 eggs
3 cups chicken stock
1 cup fresh oregano leaves (or 1 tablespoon dried oregano and 1 cup fresh flat-leaf parsley)
2 cloves garlic
1/2 cup grated Parmesan cheese
1/4 cup olive oil
1 teaspoon salt
1/2 teaspoon freshly ground pepper

The chicken

4 2-pound roasting chickens
2 heads garlic, halved
2 lemons, halved
1 bunch fresh oregano or 4 tablespoons dried oregano
4 tablespoons olive oil
1 1/2 tablespoons salt
2 teaspoons freshly ground pepper

To Make the Stuffing: Preheat the oven to 350 degrees. Break the bread into pieces and toast them on a baking sheet until they are dry and slightly brown. Remove from the oven. (Leave the oven on.) Butter the inside of a large casserole dish and set it aside. Combine the eggs and chicken stock in a large glass or ceramic bowl. Set aside. Place the fresh oregano (or dried oregano and parsley), garlic, and Parmesan cheese in the bowl of a food processor. Chop and combine them, using a pulse action. Then add the olive oil while the food processor is running. Add this mixture to the egg and chicken stock mixture. Season with salt and pepper and toss in the bread. Spoon the stuffing into the prepared casserole dish and bake for 1 hour, until the top is brown and crusty.

To Roast the Chicken: Preheat the oven to 400 degrees. Rinse the chickens and pat them dry with paper towels. Place half a head of garlic, half a lemon, and one-fourth of the oregano inside each chicken. Rub the outside of each chicken with 1 tablespoon of olive oil. Sprinkle each one with salt and pepper. Place the chickens in a large roasting pan and roast them for 1 hour. Remove from the oven and let the chickens cool for 5 minutes. Carve them and serve immediately with the piping hot stuffing.

DUANE PARK
CAFÉ

157 Duane Street (between W. Broadway & Hudson)
New York, N.Y. 10013
212-732-5555

OVEN-DRIED TOMATOES & WHIPPED WHITE BEANS

DUANE PARK CAFE

THESE TWO SIDE dishes are excellent accompaniments to the Roasted Chicken with Oregano Bruschetta Stuffing as well as other main meat dishes. The oven-dried tomatoes are also very tasty on their own. They can be made in advance and stored at room temperature. Plan ahead so you have enough time to soak the beans beforehand (see page 165). Choose any variety of dried white bean, such as Great Northern beans. You can make the final preparation to the whipped beans while the chicken (or other meat dish) is roasting.

SERVES EIGHT

The oven-dried tomatoes
16 plum tomatoes
2 teaspoons sugar
1 teaspoon salt
1/2 teaspoon freshly ground pepper
2 tablespoons olive oil

The whipped beans
1/2 pound dried white beans, soaked (see page 165) and rinsed
1 teaspoon salt
1/2 teaspoon freshly ground pepper
1/2 cup olive oil
cooking liquid from beans

To Prepare the Tomatoes: Preheat the oven to 325 degrees. Cut each tomato in half lengthwise and place the halves cut-side-up on a baking sheet. Sprinkle them with the sugar, salt, and pepper. Drizzle olive oil on top and bake the tomatoes for 1 1/2 hours, or until they are dried.

To Prepare the Whipped Beans: Place the soaked beans in a medium-sized saucepan. Cover them with cold water and place the pan over high heat. Bring the water to a boil. Then lower the heat, add salt and pepper, cover the pan, and simmer for 30 to 45 minutes, until the beans are soft. (Add more water if necessary.)

Remove from the heat. Drain the beans, reserving about 1 cup of cooking liquid. Purée the beans in a food processor until smooth. While the food processor is running, add the olive oil in a steady stream. Add some of the cooking liquid as needed, and continue to process until the beans have the consistency of mashed potatoes. Serve immediately.

DUANE PARK CAFE

QUINCE FRITTERS WITH CIDER CARAMEL & WALNUT BRITTLE ICE CREAM

QUINCE ARE FRAGRANT, applelike fruit that are available in the autumn. The ice cream that accompanies the fritters is delicious and simple to prepare.

SERVES EIGHT

The walnut brittle ice cream

1 cup walnuts, coarsely chopped

1 1/2 cups sugar

2 cups milk

1 2-inch piece vanilla bean, split in half lengthwise, or 1 tablespoon vanilla extract

9 egg yolks

1 cup heavy cream

1 cup crème fraîche

The quince fritters and the cider caramel

4 fresh quince—peeled, quartered, and cored

1 quart apple cider

1 cup flour

1/4 teaspoon salt

1/2 teaspoon baking powder

1/2 teaspoon cinnamon

2 tablespoons lemon zest (about 2 lemons)

1 to 2 quarts vegetable oil for deep-frying

1 cup beer

2 tablespoons vanilla extract

additional flour for dusting

1/4 cup confectioners' sugar

To Make the Walnut Brittle: Preheat the oven to 350 degrees. Toast the walnuts on a baking sheet for 5 minutes. Remove from the oven. Meanwhile, caramelize 1/2 cup of the sugar in a heavy-bottomed skillet on medium heat until it turns a rich golden brown. Remove from the heat and immediately pour the caramelized sugar over the toasted walnuts. Allow the brittle to cool and solidify. Then transfer it to a chopping board and coarsely chop it. Set aside.

To Make the Ice Cream: Bring the milk just to a boil in a heavy-bottomed, nonreactive saucepan with the vanilla bean. Remove from the heat. Meanwhile, whisk the remaining 1 cup of sugar into the egg yolks in a large nonreactive bowl. Whisk the warmed milk into the yolk mixture. Return the mixture to the saucepan and cook slowly over medium heat, stirring with a wooden spoon until the custard thickens and coats the back of the spoon. (Be careful not to let it boil.)

Remove from the heat and transfer the custard to a stainless steel bowl set in an ice bath. Allow the custard to cool completely. Remove the vanilla bean and stir in the cream and crème fraîche. (If you are using vanilla extract, stir it in at this time.) Transfer the mixture to an ice cream maker and process, following the manufacturer's instructions, until the ice cream is almost firm but still soft enough to stir. Add the chopped walnut brittle, and complete processing. Store the ice cream in the freezer until firm.

To Prepare the Caramel: Slice the quince into 1/2-inch slices and place them in a medium-sized non-reactive saucepan. Cover them with the apple cider and cook over medium heat for about 30 minutes, or until the fruit is soft enough to pierce with a paring knife. Transfer the fruit to a bowl, cover it, and set it aside. Increase the heat to high and continue cooking the cider, reducing it to the consistency of thin caramel. (Should it get too thick, whisk in more water to thin it.) Remove from the heat. Pass the caramel through a fine sieve, into a small bowl, and set it aside.

To Make the Fritters: Mix together the flour, salt, baking powder, cinnamon, and the lemon zest in a large nonreactive mixing bowl. Set aside. Heat the vegetable oil in a wok or deep skillet until it is hot. Whisk the beer and vanilla extract into the dry ingredients. Dust the quince slices with additional flour and then coat them in the fritter batter. Fry the fritters on both sides until they are golden brown. Remove from the hot oil and place them on paper towels to drain.

To Serve: Dust the fritters with confectioners' sugar and serve them hot, with the ice cream and caramel.

EL TEDDY'S

Fall Menu

❧

TURBAN SQUASH
& ANCHO CHILE
SOUP

WILD
MUSHROOM &
HUITLACOCHE
QUESADILLAS
WITH MIXED
GREENS

WARM APPLE
EMPANADAS WITH
ORANGE
HIBISCUS SAUCE

TURBAN SQUASH & ANCHO CHILE SOUP

TURBAN SQUASH IS available at farmer's markets and grocery stores in the fall. You may substitute butternut squash, which is available all winter long. You may also substitute Mexican chiles for the ancho chiles, but use only one or two because they generally are larger. This soup will keep for three days in the refrigerator or for three months in the freezer.

SERVES EIGHT

3 dried ancho chiles, stems and seeds removed

2 leeks, tops removed

2 tablespoons olive oil

1 medium-sized onion, diced small

4 cloves garlic, minced

salt

freshly ground white pepper

2 1/2 pounds turban squash—peeled, seeded, and cut in chunks

2 golden delicious apples—peeled, cored, and cut in chunks

8 cups light chicken stock or water

1 bunch green onions (tops only), minced, for garnish

6 to 8 tablespoons crème fraîche for garnish (optional)

Lightly toast the ancho chiles in a dry sauté pan over medium heat for 5 minutes. Remove from the heat. Place the chiles in a bowl and cover them with warm water for 30 minutes.

Cut the leeks in half lengthwise. Rinse them well and cut them into thin slices. Set aside. Heat the oil in a large, heavy-bottomed saucepan over medium heat and sauté the onions and leeks until they are soft. Add the garlic, salt, and pepper and continue to sauté until the mixture is lightly browned. Add the squash, apples, chiles, and stock or water. Increase the heat to high and bring the liquid to a boil. Reduce the heat and simmer for 20 minutes until the mixture is very soft. Remove from the heat. Purée the soup in batches in a blender or food processor and strain it through a fine sieve. Adjust the seasoning.

To Serve: Serve the soup hot, garnished with green onions and a dollop of crème fraîche.

†WINE SUGGESTION

Chef Peter Klein recommends serving Negro Modelo, a Mexican amber beer, throughout the meal.

EL TEDDY'S — WILD MUSHROOM & *HUITLACOCHE* QUESADILLAS WITH MIXED GREENS

HUITLACOCHE IS A corn fungus that is becoming more widely available at specialty markets. To order by mail, refer to the Sources Guide (page 169). This recipe can also be made without the *huitlacoche.* Simply substitute an equal amount of mushrooms for this ingredient. You can use any variety of mushrooms for this recipe, including chanterelles, shiitakes, oyster mushrooms, creminis, or portobellos.

SERVES EIGHT

2 tablespoons olive oil

4 cloves garlic, minced

2 large shallots, minced

2 red bell peppers, seeded and diced

1 pound fresh *huitlacoche*, coarsely chopped

1 pound fresh mushrooms, thinly sliced

hot-pepper sauce, chile sauce, or Tabasco sauce

salt

freshly ground black pepper

4 tablespoons fresh cilantro, chopped

1 pound Monterey jack cheese, grated

12 ounces firm goats' milk cheese, crumbled

8 10-inch flour tortillas

8 handfuls Mesclun or bitter greens, washed and dried

1/2 cup olive oil

1/4 cup vinegar or lime juice

Heat the olive oil in a large sauté pan over medium heat. Sauté the garlic, shallots, and bell peppers until they begin to soften. Increase the heat to high and add the *huitlacoche* and mushrooms, cooking until the liquid is completely reduced. Remove from the heat. Season to taste with hot-pepper sauce, salt, and pepper. Let the mixture cool to room temperature. Stir in the cilantro and set aside.

Combine the two cheeses in a small bowl. Set aside. Place one tortilla in a skillet over medium heat. Top with one-eighth of the mushroom mixture and one-eighth of the cheese mixture. Fold the tortilla in half with a metal spatula. Cook it on both sides until it is lightly browned and the cheese melts. Remove the quesadilla from the pan, cut it into wedges, transfer it to a warm serving plate, and keep it warm.

Repeat with the remaining ingredients.

To Serve: Place a handful of Mesclun on each dinner plate. Dress the salad with the oil and vinegar or lime juice. Arrange the quesadilla wedges on the plate, slightly overlapping the greens. Serve immediately.

<table>
</table>

EL TEDDY'S

WARM APPLE EMPANADAS WITH ORANGE HIBISCUS SAUCE

WITH THIS RECIPE, you can present a hot dessert with only minor last-minute preparation. The dough and filling can be prepared well in advance. You can also assemble the empanadas and store them unbaked in an airtight container in the freezer for up to one month. Serve the dessert straight from the oven, with vanilla ice cream and Mexican hot chocolate, which contains canela (a variety of cinnamon) and almonds. Chef Klein prefers to use Ibarra Mexican Chocolate, a brand that is widely available in the United States.

MAKES 10 TO 12 EMPANADAS

The dough
2 1/4 cups flour
2 teaspoons baking powder
pinch of salt
3/4 cup brown sugar
8 tablespoons unsalted butter, softened to room
    temperature
1 egg yolk
3 tablespoons mascarpone or softened cream cheese
3 to 4 tablespoons water

The apple filling
4 cooking apples (such as Granny Smith)—
    peeled, cored, and diced very small
1/4 cup brown sugar
1 tablespoon cornstarch
2 tablespoons ground cinnamon
1 teaspoon ground coriander seed
1 tablespoon lemon juice
1/4 cup water

The egg wash
1 egg, lightly beaten
1/4 cup water

The orange hibiscus sauce
1 Granny Smith apple—peeled, cored, and coarsely
    chopped
1/3 cup sugar
1 cup hibiscus tea
6 tablespoons freshly squeezed orange juice

To Make the Dough: Combine the flour, baking powder, salt, and brown sugar in a large mixing bowl or the bowl of a food processor. Add the butter, egg yolk, and mascarpone or cream cheese, and blend until the mixture forms a soft ball. (If the dough doesn't stick together, add water, 1 tablespoon at a time, while processing.) Wrap the dough in plastic wrap and store it in the refrigerator or freezer. (If you freeze the dough, allow plenty of time for it to thaw out before using.)

To Make the Filling: Place all of the ingredients for the filling in a heavy-bottomed saucepan and cook over medium-low heat for 15 minutes, or until the apples begin to soften. (If the mixture becomes too dry or thick, add a few tablespoons of water, one at a time.) Remove from the heat and let the mixture cool completely.

To Assemble the Empanadas: Preheat the oven to 325 degrees. Grease a large baking sheet or line it with parchment paper. Roll the dough on a floured surface to a thickness of 1/2-inch. Cut out 4-inch circles using a cookie cutter.

Place 1 generous tablespoon of apple filling in the center of each circle and fold the circle in half. Crimp the edges with a fork. Place the empanadas on a baking sheet. (If you want to store them in the refrigerator or freezer at this point, seal them in an airtight container, separating the layers with waxed paper.) Mix the lightly beaten egg with the water. Brush each empanada with this mixture and bake for 20 to 25 minutes until golden brown. Meanwhile, prepare the orange hibiscus sauce.

To Make the Sauce: Cook the apples and sugar in the tea until the apples are very soft. Purée the mixture in a blender and let it cool. Add the orange juice to the purée and stir. (If you are making the sauce in advance, transfer it to a tightly lidded glass jar. Refrigerate for up to three days. Return to room temperature before serving.)

To Serve: On each of 8 warm dessert plates, ladle some of the sauce. Place two empanadas on each plate. Serve with a scoop of ice cream.

MONTRACHET

Fall Menu

❦

GRILLED QUAIL
SALAD WITH
BALSAMIC
VINAIGRETTE

SALMON WITH
LENTILS & RED
WINE SAUCE

HOT & COLD
CHOCOLATE
TRUFFLE TORTE
WITH RASPBERRY
PURÉE

GRILLED QUAIL SALAD WITH BALSAMIC VINAIGRETTE

THIS IS A lovely and uncomplicated dish for which all of the preparation, except the grilling, is done a day ahead. Although it's a wonderful choice for those last autumn days of outdoor grilling, the quail can be broiled successfully in an indoor oven. If you are not able to find boneless quail at your local market, you can bone them yourself or purchase them by mail. (Refer to the Sources Guide on page 169.) You can also substitute four chicken breasts for the quail.

SERVES SIX

---

4 tablespoons minced shallots (about 2 large
    shallots)
2/3 cup balsamic vinegar
1 1/2 cups olive oil
salt
freshly ground pepper
6 quail, breastbones removed
12 medium new potatoes
6 handfuls Mesclun salad greens

To Marinate the Quail: Combine the shallots and balsamic vinegar in a medium-sized bowl. Slowly whisk in the olive oil to emulsify. Season with salt and pepper. Set aside this vinaigrette.

Place the quail in a nonreactive bowl and pour half of the vinaigrette on top. Cover and refrigerate overnight. Reserve the remaining vinaigrette for the potatoes and greens.

To Prepare the Potatoes: Peel the potatoes and place them in a large saucepan with water. Add a pinch of salt and bring the water to a boil over high heat. Cook until tender. Remove from the heat. Drain the potatoes and set them aside. Allow them to cool slightly. Cut the potatoes into 1/4-inch slices and marinate them overnight in 1/2 cup of the vinaigrette. (Reserve the rest of the vinaigrette for the greens.)

To Grill the Quail: The next day, remove the quail from the vinaigrette. Lightly grill or broil the quail, skin side down, for 8 to 10 minutes. (Halfway through the cooking time, turn the quail over and grill it on the other side.) Meanwhile, gently heat the potatoes in the vinaigrette in a saucepan over low heat until they are warm. Remove from the heat.

†WINE SUGGESTION

Daniel Johnnes, Wine Director at Montrachet, has selected the following wines to be enjoyed with this meal: with the Grilled Quail Salad, a Meursault-Charmes 1989, Domaine de Comtes Lafon; with the Salmon with Lentils, a Volnay-Champans 1990, Domaine Marquis Angerville; with the Hot & Cold Chocolate Truffle, a Blandy's 10-year-old Malmsey Madeira.

To Serve: Toss the Mesclun greens with the remaining vinaigrette. Arrange the greens in the center of 6 salad plates. Distribute the potatoes, placing them around the greens. Slice the quail breasts and arrange the slices and the legs and thighs around the greens. Serve immediately.

MONTRACHET SALMON WITH LENTILS & RED WINE SAUCE

THE RICH CREAMY lentils in this dish provide a flavorful bed for the simply prepared salmon. The lentils and the sauce can be prepared earlier in the day; reheat the sauce before serving.

SERVES SIX

The creamed lentils
3/4 cup dried green lentils
3/4 cup finely diced bacon
2 shallots, minced
1 clove garlic, minced
1 pint heavy cream
1 teaspoon finely chopped fresh thyme
1 teaspoon finely chopped fresh marjoram
1/4 teaspoon salt
freshly ground white pepper

The sauce
2 tablespoons olive oil
1/2 pound salmon bones, cut in pieces
1 clove garlic, finely chopped
2 carrots, diced

2 stalks celery, diced
1 leek, finely chopped
1 sprig fresh tarragon
1 sprig fresh thyme
1 bottle (24 ounces) red table wine
1 cup chicken stock
1/4 teaspoon salt
1/4 teaspoon freshly ground pepper
3 tablespoons butter

The salmon
2 pounds center-cut salmon fillet
1/2 pound *haricots verts*, quickly steamed,
   for garnish

To Prepare the Lentils: Blanch the lentils for 10 minutes in a pot of boiling water. Drain and set aside.

In a large sauté pan, fry the bacon until it is lightly browned. Add the shallots and garlic, and sauté for 2 minutes, until they are tender and translucent. Add the lentils, cream, thyme, and marjoram. Simmer about 15 minutes, until the

MONTRACHET
239 West Broadway • in TriBeCa • New York, N.Y. 10013

DANIEL JOHNNES   212 219-2777
Wine Director / Sommelier

lentils are tender and the mixture resembles a thick soup. Remove from the heat. Season with salt and pepper. Set aside.

To Make the Sauce. Heat the olive oil in a saucepan over medium heat. Add the salmon bones, garlic, carrots, celery, and leeks and cook until the vegetables are golden brown. Add the tarragon, thyme, wine, and stock. Increase the heat and

bring the sauce to a boil. Simmer for 15 to 20 minutes. Strain the sauce through a fine sieve and return it to a clean saucepan. Bring the sauce to a boil and continue cooking over high heat until it has reduced to about 3/4 cup and is slightly thickened. Remove from the heat. Add the salt and pepper, and adjust the seasoning. Whisk in the butter. (If you have made the sauce ahead of time, reheat it while the salmon is cookng, and add the butter at that time.)

To Serve: Preheat the broiler. Slice the raw salmon diagonally into long thin slices. Place 1/2 cup of the creamed lentils on each of 6 ovenproof plates. Place two slices of salmon on top, without overlapping them. Broil the salmon for about 2 minutes. Remove the plates from the broiler. Spoon the warm sauce around the salmon and garnish with *haricots verts.* Serve immediately.

HOT & COLD CHOCOLATE TRUFFLE TORTE WITH RASPBERRY PURÉE

MONTRACHET

THIS IS A dessert for chocolate lovers. The contrast of the hot and light ganache with the cold and heavy ganache creates a great textural taste sensation. Surrounded by raspberry purée and fresh berries, the torte is a visual treat as well. Although there are several steps involved, this is not a difficult dessert to prepare. The entire torte can be prepared in advance and stored in the freezer for up to one week. Pastry Chef David Blom recommends refrigerating the ganache overnight before you assemble it, to enhance the flavors. Choose two complementary flavors of liqueur or liquor; add a different flavor to each ganache.

MAKES ONE 8-INCH TORTE

The ganache
1 cup heavy cream
1 tablespoon sugar
1 pound semisweet chocolate, coarsely chopped
1 tablespoon butter
2 tablespoons bourbon, rum, brandy, Grand
    Marnier, or other liqueur

The raspberry purée
3 pints fresh red raspberries or 1 1/2 cups frozen
    unsweetened red raspberries
1/4 cup sugar
1/4 cup confectioners' sugar
fresh raspberries for garnish

To Make the Ganache: Combine the heavy cream and sugar in a heavy saucepan over high heat. Bring the cream to a boil. Meanwhile, place the chocolate in a large ceramic bowl. Pour the hot cream over the chocolate and add the butter. Gently stir until the mixture is smooth and the chocolate is completely melted.

Divide the ganache equally into two separate bowls. Add 1 tablespoon of a different liquor or liqueur to each bowl and stir each ganache to combine. Cover the bowls with plastic wrap and refrigerate them, preferably overnight or at least 30 minutes, until the chocolate solidifies.

To Assemble the Torte: Unwrap one ganache and cut it into chunks. Place it in a heatproof bowl over a pot of hot but not boiling water. Stir constantly with a rubber spatula until most of the ganache melts. Remove from the heat. Continue stirring until there are no lumps and the ganache has the consistency of mayonnaise. Pour it into an 8-inch springform pan, spreading it evenly on the bottom of the pan. Place the pan in the freezer for 20 minutes, until the ganache sets.

Meanwhile, melt the other ganache in the same method. Pour it into a mixing bowl. Beat the ganache, using an electric mixer set at medium-high speed for 5 minutes, or until it lightens noticeably in color. Pour this ganache on top of the frozen one in the springform pan. Smooth out the surface, making sure that it is even. Cover with plastic wrap and freeze until solid. Meanwhile, prepare the raspberry purée.

To Make the Raspberry Purée: Combine the raspberries and sugar and purée the mixture in a blender or food processor. Pass the purée through a fine sieve into a bowl. (You should have one cup of purée.) Cover and refrigerate until ready to serve.

To Serve: Preheat the broiler for 15 minutes. Take the pan out of the freezer and unmold the torte by rubbing a hot damp towel along the sides of the pan. Run a knife under hot water, dry it, and use it to cut the torte into 6 wedges. Remove each wedge and place it on an ovenproof serving plate. Dust the top of each torte with about 1/2 tablespoon of confectioners' sugar. Broil the torte slices for 1 to 2 minutes, until the top ganache has softened slightly. (The bottom should remain firm.) Remove from the broiler. Garnish with raspberry purée and fresh raspberries, and serve immediately.

THE ODEON

Fall Menu

❧

WARM CHICORY
SALAD WITH
SWEET GARLIC,
CROUTONS,
BACON &
ROQUEFORT
CHEESE

GRILLED STRIPED
BASS WITH
CHANTERELLES &
HARICOTS VERTS

RASPBERRY
ALMOND TART

WARM CHICORY SALAD WITH SWEET GARLIC, CROUTONS, BACON & ROQUEFORT CHEESE

THIS SALAD IS one of the Odeon's standards, and it is always a taste delight. The garlic, croutons, bacon, and dressing can all be made in advance and tossed together just before serving.

SERVES SIX

The sweet garlic
20 whole cloves garlic, peeled
1 cup milk

1 tablespoon sugar
2 tablespoons clarified butter
salt
freshly ground pepper

The croutons and bacon
1/2 pound slab bacon, cut into 1/2-inch cubes
1 cup 1/2-inch cubes bread, crust removed
3 to 4 tablespoons rendered bacon fat

The mustard dressing
1 shallot, finely diced
1 tablespoon Dijon mustard
2 tablespoons red wine vinegar
5 tablespoons extra virgin olive oil
pinch of salt
1/4 teaspoon freshly ground pepper

The salad
1 large head chicory (curly endive), washed and
  dried
1/2 cup Roquefort cheese, crumbled
freshly ground pepper

To Prepare the Sweet Garlic: Place the garlic and milk in a heavy saucepan over medium-high heat, and bring the milk to a boil. Boil for 3 minutes. Remove from the heat. Discard the milk, reserving the garlic. Combine the sugar and butter over medium heat. Add the garlic and cook until the cloves are soft and lightly caramelized. Season with salt and pepper. Set the sweet garlic aside.

To Prepare the Croutons and Bacon: Preheat the oven to 350 degrees. Meanwhile, fry the bacon in a skillet until it is crisp but not dry. Remove from the heat and place the bacon on paper towels. Pour off all but 3 to 4 tablespoons of the rendered bacon fat. Add the cubed bread to the pan and toss to coat. Season with salt and pepper

†WINE SUGGESTION

Chef Lyle recommends serving a Bouzeron 1992 Aligoté White Burgundy with this meal.

and transfer the bread cubes to a baking sheet. Bake for 5 minutes, or until they are lightly browned. Set aside.

To Make the Dressing: Mix the shallots, mustard, and vinegar together. Gradually whisk in the olive oil until the liquid is well blended. Season with salt and pepper. Set aside.

To Serve: Tear the chicory leaves into small pieces. Place them in a serving bowl and set aside at room temperature.

Heat the bacon in a small, heavy-bottomed skillet over medium-high heat. Add the croutons and then the dressing. Toss for 2 seconds, pour it over the salad greens, and toss thoroughly. (Don't overcook the dressing or the mustard will lose its flavor.)

Serve the salad on individual plates, topped with crumbled Roquefort cheese, sweet garlic, and freshly ground pepper to taste.

THE ODEON	GRILLED STRIPED BASS WITH CHANTERELLES & *HARICOTS VERTS*

WILD STRIPED BASS are available again in early September. Although no other fish comes close to matching the flavor of wild striped bass, halibut fillets served in this manner give satisfying results. In this recipe, the mushrooms are marinated in their own liquid and should be allowed to sit for a few hours so the flavors have a chance to develop. If the mushrooms are large, quarter them. Otherwise, leave them whole. Chef Lyle prefers to serve this dish with *pousse pieds* (also known as sea beans), which is a beautiful green seaweed. If you can find them, use the *pousse pieds* instead of the *haricots verts* for the true Odeon experience.

SERVES SIX

The mushrooms
1 1/3 cups olive oil
2 pounds fresh chanterelles, cleaned
1/4 teaspoon salt
1/4 teaspoon freshly ground pepper
1 1/2 tablespoons chopped fresh thyme
4 large cloves garlic, finely chopped
4 large shallots, finely chopped
3 tablespoons sherry vinegar
4 tablespoons fresh lemon juice

The striped bass
6 7-ounce portions striped bass, scaled and filleted
olive oil
salt
freshly ground pepper

The haricots verts
1/2 cup butter
3 shallots, diced
1 1/2 pounds *haricots verts* or *pousse pieds*, blanched
salt
freshly ground pepper
1 tablespoon fresh lemon juice

Garnish
1 bunch chervil
6 lemon wedges

To Prepare the Mushrooms: Heat 2/3 cup of olive oil in a sauté pan until it is hot. Add the mushrooms, salt, and pepper. Cook for 5 minutes over medium-high heat. Add the thyme, garlic, half of the chopped shallots, and the vinegar, and sauté for 1 more minute. Remove from the heat and let the mushrooms cool. Add the remaining 2/3 cup of olive oil, the remaining chopped shallots, and the lemon juice. Set aside for at least 2 hours, or until you are ready to serve the dish. Gently reheat the mushrooms over low heat while you grill the fish.

To Grill the Fish: Prepare the grill. Rub the fish on both sides with a little olive oil and season lightly with salt and pepper. Grill the fish for 5 to 6 minutes, or until done, turning it to make a cross-

hatch pattern. (Halfway through the grilling time, flip the fish over to cook the other side. Make a crosshatch pattern on this side, too.) Remove from the grill and keep the fish warm.

To Prepare the Haricots Verts: While the fish are grilling, melt the butter in a medium-sized saucepan. Add the diced shallots, cover, and sweat the shallots (see page 166) until they are soft. Add the *haricots verts* and sauté them quickly over high heat. Season with salt, pepper, and lemon juice. (If you are using *pousse pieds*, do not add any salt.)

To Serve: Place the grilled bass and *haricots verts* on warm dinner plates. Spoon the reheated mushrooms over the fish and vegetables. Garnish with sprigs of chervil and lemon wedges. Serve immediately.

THE ODEON RASPBERRY ALMOND TART

RESTAURANTS OFTEN GREET their guests with a tempting dessert tray, enticing the taste buds and providing a gentle warning to leave room for dessert. This tart recipe is simple to make and allows for a professional presentation of just such a dessert. The tart can be fully prepared up to one day in advance, covered, and refrigerated until an hour before serving.

MAKES ONE 10-INCH TART

The crust
1/2 cup almond paste, packed (1/4 pound)
4 teaspoons sugar
4 tablespoons butter, softened to room temperature
2 tablespoons plus 2 teaspoons cake flour
1 large egg
2 teaspoons vanilla extract

The topping
1/3 cup raspberry preserves
1 to 1 1/2 pints fresh raspberries
1/2 pint heavy cream
1 tablespoon raspberry liqueur
1 teaspoon vanilla extract

To Prepare the Crust: Preheat the oven to 400 degrees. Lightly butter a 10 inch springform pan. Combine the almond paste and sugar in a mixing bowl or the bowl of a food processor. Add the butter, flour, egg, and vanilla. Spread the mixture into the prepared pan and bake for 10 to 12 minutes, or until light brown and firm to the touch. Remove from the oven. Unmold the tart crust onto a serving plate and let it cool.

To Top the Crust: Bring the raspberry preserves to a boil in a small saucepan. Remove from the heat and pass the liquefied preserves through a sieve. Spread the preserves evenly over the crust. Arrange the fresh raspberries in concentric circles, upright, to completely cover the preserves. Cut the tart into wedges and place each slice on a dessert plate. Whip the cream with the liqueur and the vanilla extract. Serve a dollop of whipped cream on each slice of tart.

WINTER

ARQUA

Winter Menu

❧

PASTA FAGIOLI

SAUTÉED
RADICCHIO WITH
MELTED *Taleggio*
& FONTINA
CHEESES

OSSO BUCO WITH
SAFFRON
RISOTTO

APPLE TART

PASTA FAGIOLI

THIS SOUP IS a wonderful start to a hearty meal, or it can be served as a meal itself with a crusty bread, cheese, and a salad. The soup can be prepared in advance and stored in the refrigerator for up to four days, or in the freezer for up to one month, but add the cooked pasta just before serving. To prepare a vegetarian version of this soup, substitute the bean cooking liquid for the chicken stock.

SERVES SIX

1 pound (2 cups) dried white beans, soaked (see page 165) and drained
3/4 cup extra virgin olive oil
8 cups cold water
6 to 8 large fresh sage leaves
4 bay leaves
1 teaspoon salt
3/4 teaspoon freshly ground pepper
1 large onion, finely chopped
2 medium carrots, coarsely chopped
2 stalks celery, coarsely chopped
2 medium zucchini, coarsely chopped
8 cups chicken stock
1 pound #4 tubular hollow dried pasta (or other short, hollow pasta)
additional extra virgin olive oil for garnish
freshly grated Parmesan cheese

Place the beans in a stockpot and add 1/2 cup of the olive oil, the water, sage, bay leaves, salt, and pepper. Cook over low heat for 1 1/2 to 2 hours, or until the beans are soft. Remove from the heat and set aside to cool.

Heat the remaining 1/4 cup of olive oil in a large, heavy-bottomed saucepan over medium heat. Add the onions and cook for a few minutes, until they are soft. Add the carrots and celery and continue to cook for a few more minutes. Then add the zucchini and continue cooking for 20 to 30 minutes, until all of the vegetables are tender. Remove the sage and bay leaves from the beans, and discard. Pour off the cooking liquid. (Reserve if you want to make the soup without chicken stock.) Add half of the beans to the vegetables.

†WINE SUGGESTION

Leo Pulito, proprietor and chef of Arqua, recommends serving a Dolcetto to accompany both the Pasta Fagioli *and the* Sautéed Radicchio. *With the Osso Buco he recommends a Barolo, 1989, 1990, or 1991, preferably one produced by Ainaldi. With dessert a young Dindarello, produced by Maculan.*

Pour the vegetable and bean mixture into the bowl of a food processor and purée the mixture using the pulse action about 8 times. (Do not overpurée.) Pour this purée into the stockpot with the remaining beans. Add the chicken stock (or bean cooking liquid) and stir to blend. Keep the soup warm while you make the pasta.

Bring water to boil in a large saucepan. Cook the pasta until it is al dente. Drain and add the pasta to the soup.

To Serve: Splash some olive oil into each bowlful of soup and sprinkle Parmesan cheese on top. Serve immediately.

SAUTÉED RADICCHIO WITH MELTED *TALEGGIO* & FONTINA CHEESES

ARQUA

THE PREPARATION FOR this first course can take place a few hours in advance. It takes only five minutes to cook the dish, but it should be served immediately. Chef Pulito suggests serving the stuffed radicchio on a bed of Belgian endive, shredded carrots, and thinly sliced fennel. You can also serve it on a bed of assorted crisp vegetables and salad greens to complement the deep red of the radicchio.

SERVES SIX

3 large heads radicchio
1/2 pound *taleggio* cheese, divided into 6 equal portions
1/2 pound Italian fontina cheese, divided into 6 equal portions
1/3 cup olive oil
1 teaspoon salt
1/2 teaspoon freshly ground pepper
3 heads Belgian endive, separated into leaves
3 carrots, shredded
1 head fennel, thinly sliced
olive oil
1 lemon

Cut the hard core out of the bottom of each radicchio head and gently remove the leaves. Wash and dry the leaves. Stack them into 12 separate piles. Place one portion of *taleggio* in each of 6 piles of radicchio leaves, wrapping the leaves snugly and folding the edges in. Tie each bundle securely around four sides (as you would a package) using kitchen twine. Set aside. Repeat with the 6 remaining piles of leaves, filling each pile with a portion of fontina cheese. Tie each bundle securely. Keep the *taleggio*-filled bundles separate from the fontina-filled ones.

Generously coat each prepared radicchio bundle with olive oil. Season with salt and pepper. Heat a skillet over medium-high heat and sear the radicchio bundles for 2 minutes on each side. (Again, keep the bundles separate according to the cheese filling.) Remove the bundles from the pan and place them on a warm dish. Remove the twine.

To Serve: Arrange the endive, carrots, and fennel on 6 salad plates. Place one *taleggio*-filled bundle and one fontina-filled bundle on each plate. Drizzle each one with olive oil and a squeeze of lemon juice. Serve immediately.

ARQUA — OSSO BUCO WITH SAFFRON RISOTTO

CHEF PULITO'S OSSO buco is cooked in the oven rather than on the stove. The finely chopped vegetables make a savory and hearty sauce for the meat. You can make this dish one day in advance, store it in the refrigerator, and reheat it in the oven while you prepare the saffron risotto.

SERVES SIX

The osso buco
6 2 1/2-inch-thick veal shanks
2 tablespoons butter
2 tablespoons olive oil
3 medium carrots, finely chopped
3 stalks celery, finely chopped
1 large onion, finely chopped
3 cloves garlic, finely chopped
1 cup soy or corn oil
1/4 to 1/2 cup flour for dusting shanks
1 cup white wine

RISTORANTE

ARQUÀ

281 Church Street, New York, New York 10013   212/334 1888

2 tablespoons tomato paste

pinch of salt

pinch of freshly ground pepper

The saffron risotto

10 threads saffron

1 quart chicken stock

1/2 medium onion, finely chopped

1 tablespoon olive oil

2 1/2 cups Arborio rice

1/2 cup dry white wine

2 tablespoons butter

1/2 cup freshly grated Parmesan cheese

Garnish

1/4 cup chopped flat-leaf parsley

rind of 1 lemon, coarsely chopped or grated

To Prepare the Osso Buco: Trim the fat from the veal shanks, and tie them tightly in the middle with kitchen twine. Set them aside. Cook the butter, olive oil, carrots, celery, onions, and garlic in a large ovenproof casserole over medium heat for about 6 minutes, or until vegetables are soft and tender. Remove from the heat and set aside.

Preheat the oven to 425 degrees. In a large skillet, heat the soy or corn oil over medium-high heat. Dust the veal shanks with flour. Sear them on all sides in the hot oil. Remove them with a slotted spoon and blot them with paper towels.

Place the veal shanks side by side in the casserole with the vegetables. Add the wine and bring the liquid to a boil. Lower the heat and simmer for 10 minutes. Stir in the tomato paste, salt, and pepper. Add enough water to reach a level of three-fourths the height of the veal shanks. Cover the casserole and place it in the oven. Bake for 1 1/2 hours or until the meat feels tender and the vegetables have cooked to a rich sauce. Remove from the oven.

To Make the Risotto: Melt the saffron in the chicken stock in a saucepan over medium heat. Set aside.

In a large saucepan, sear the onions in olive oil over medium-high heat for 2 to 3 minutes, being careful not to burn them. Stir in the rice and wine, and cook, stirring continuously, until the wine evaporates. Lower the heat and add enough chicken stock to cover the rice. Stir and cook until the rice absorbs the stock. Add the remaining chicken stock, a ladleful at a time, stirring after each addition and allowing the rice to absorb the

stock each time. (This will take about 20 minutes.) Stir in the butter and then the cheese. Turn off the heat, cover the pot, and allow the rice to rest for 5 minutes before serving.

To Serve: Carefully remove the twine from each veal shank. Make a ring of risotto on each plate. Place a veal shank in the middle of the risotto ring. Spoon the vegetable sauce over the meat, and garnish with parsley and lemon rind. Serve immediately.

ARQUA	APPLE TART

APPLES ARE ONE of the most reliable winter fruits. Chef Pulito recommends using Granny Smith apples for this tart. You can also mix Granny Smiths with other hard, flavorful apples. When forming the crust in the tart pan, make sure that the edges are even in thickness so they will brown evenly.

MAKES ONE 10-INCH TART

The crust

1 cup all-purpose flour

1 cup cake flour

pinch of salt

1 teaspoon grated lemon rind

1 teaspoon grated orange rind

3/4 cup cold butter

2 tablespoons sugar

1 teaspoon vanilla extract

4 tablespoons cold water

The filling

1 tablespoon sugar

1/2 teaspoon cinnamon

4 Granny Smith apples

2 tablespoons butter, cut into 8 pieces

The glaze

1/2 cup apricot jam

1/4 cup water

To Prepare the Crust: Sift together the flours and salt. Then stir in the grated rind. Cut the butter into the flour mixture with a pastry blender or with your fingers (or with a food processor, using the pulse action), until the mixture resembles coarse meal. Add the sugar and combine. Mix together the vanilla and water and add this to the flour mixture, blending with a fork and your fingers until it forms a loose dough. Pat the dough into a ball, flatten it slightly, and wrap it in plastic wrap. Refrigerate the dough for at least 30 minutes. Meanwhile, you can prepare the filling.

To Make the Filling: Combine the sugar and cinnamon in a small bowl and set it aside.

Peel and core the apples. Cut them into 1/16-inch slices. Set aside.

Preheat the oven to 400 degrees. Remove the pastry from the refrigerator. Using the palm of your hand and your fingers, press the pastry into a 10-inch tart pan with a removable bottom. Flatten the top edge so it is level with the top of the pan.

Arrange the apples in the pastry shell by overlapping them slightly in concentric circles, beginning around the edge. Make a second layer of apples in the same way. Sprinkle the combined cinnamon and sugar generously over the top. Dot the top of the tart with butter. Bake the tart for 40 to 45 minutes, or until the crust is an even light golden color. Remove from the oven and place on a wire rack to cool. Meanwhile, make the glaze.

To Glaze the Tart: Heat the apricot jam with the water in a small saucepan over medium heat. Cook until the jam liquefies. Generously brush it over the slightly cooled tart to glaze. (Avoid putting any chunks of apricot on the tart.)

To Serve: Serve the tart warm or at room temperature with a dollop of whipped cream or vanilla ice cream.

COOKBOOK

BAROCCO

Winter Menu

❧

FENNEL &
PARMIGIANO
SALAD

FETTUCINE WITH
RABBIT, SQUAB &
BLACK OLIVES

POACHED PEARS
WITH
ZABAGLIONE
CREAM

FENNEL &
PARMIGIANO
SALAD

FENNEL IS AN anise-flavored vegetable with the fresh crisp bite of celery. It is eaten raw in *pinzimonio*, the traditional Tuscan crudités in which raw vegetables are dipped in seasoned olive oil. For this salad, the fennel bulb is sliced paper-thin, rendering the anise flavor very subtle. It is one of the most popular salads served at Barocco.

Although fresh fennel is increasingly available year-round, it is a winter-spring vegetable. Choose large, firm, white bulbs; brown marks and bruising are a sign of age. Choose small-leafed arugula, bright green in color.

SERVES SIX

1 large or 2 small bulbs fennel
6 tablespoons extra virgin olive oil
salt
freshly ground pepper
3 bunches arugula, washed and stemmed
1 tablespoon red wine vinegar
1/4 pound Parmesan cheese, crust removed

Trim away any brown spots and the hard bottom of the fennel bulb. Cut the bulb in half lengthwise. Slice it crosswise very thin, using a meat slicer or food processor. Distribute the fennel among 6 dinner plates. Lightly dress it with 2 tablespoons of the olive oil and a sprinkling of salt and pepper. Set aside. In a large bowl, toss the arugula with the remaining 4 tablespoons of olive oil, vinegar, salt, and pepper. Arrange a handful of arugula over each bed of fennel.

To Serve: Using the shaving side of a hand-held cheese grater or vegetable peeler, shave 5 or 6 slices of Parmesan onto the arugula and serve immediately.

BAROCCO FETTUCINE WITH RABBIT, SQUAB & BLACK OLIVES

THIS HEARTY DISH typifies the Tuscan-inspired cuisine featured at Barocco. Chef Prosperi regularly makes this dish with pappardelle. Because this pasta is not readily available, we have substituted fettucine. The sauce is not difficult to prepare. Initial cooking will take one-and-a-half hours.

†WINE SUGGESTION

Daniel Emerman, proprietor of Barocco, recommends a Carmignano, 1989, produced by Villa Il Poggiolo to be served throughout the meal.

However, you can make it as much as three days in advance, store it in the refrigerator, and reheat it before serving. This recipe calls for cooking the vegetables and meats together while adding a portion of hearty dry red wine every ten minutes. This caramelizes the vegetables and turns them a deep, almost burnt, color and provides a flavor that is essential to the dish. If you cannot get fresh rabbit and squab in your local markets, check with the suppliers listed in the Sources Guide (page 169).

SERVES SIX

3 tablespoons extra virgin olive oil
2 tablespoons butter
1 cup finely chopped celery
1 cup finely chopped carrot
1 cup finely chopped red onion
4 cloves garlic
1 sprig rosemary
1 saddle of rabbit with bones
1 whole squab, liver reserved
1/2 teaspoon salt
1 teaspoon freshly ground pepper
1 cup dry red wine
1 28-ounce can plum tomatoes with juice and
    basil
1 cube or package beef or chicken bouillon
1/3 cup pitted and coarsely chopped Niçoise
    black olives
1 1/2 pounds fettucine or pappardelle
2 tablespoons unsalted butter
3/4 cup freshly grated Parmesan cheese

Heat the olive oil and butter in a large, heavy-bottomed pot over medium-high heat. Stir in the celery, carrots, and red onions. Lower the heat, and cook the vegetables for 10 to 15 minutes, until they are slightly golden.

Meanwhile, mince the garlic and rosemary together, and stir them into the vegetables. Add the rabbit, squab, salt, and pepper. Cover and stir. Continue cooking over low heat for 10 minutes.

Remove the cover and brown the rabbit and squab over medium heat, turning them occasionally and stirring the vegetables. Continue cooking for 1 hour, adding 2 tablespoons of wine every 10 minutes or so to loosen the pan juices.

Remove the rabbit and set it aside. Add the squab liver to the pot and continue to cook for 10 minutes. Remove the liver and set it aside.

Continue cooking the squab another 10 minutes, until the leg moves easily in the joint. Remove the squab and set it aside with the rabbit and liver, and allow them to cool. Remove the pot from the heat and set it aside.

Cut the meat from the bones and return the bones to the pot. Chop the meat and the liver into 1/2-inch cubes and set aside. Purée the tomatoes in a food mill or food processor. Add the puréed tomatoes and bouillon to the pot. Simmer over medium heat for 20 minutes without stirring, allowing the oil to separate from the sauce.

Remove the bones, add the olives, and cook for 5 minutes. Remove from the heat, add the chopped meats, and adjust the seasoning. (If you are not serving the dish immediately, allow the sauce to cool, and then store it in the refrigerator.)

To Serve: Bring a large pot of salted water to a rolling boil and cook the fettucine or pappardelle al dente. Drain the pasta and add it to the warm sauce with the unsalted butter and Parmesan cheese. Mix gently and serve immediately.

BAROCCO POACHED PEARS WITH ZABAGLIONE CREAM

THE CHILLED PINK pears poached in port and covered with creamy yellow zabaglione make a wonderful dessert presentation. Both the pears and the zabaglione cream can be prepared one day in advance and kept in the refrigerator. Cooking time varies with the ripeness of the pears, so try to choose pears of uniform ripeness.

SERVES SIX

The poached pears
6 Bartlett pears (firm but not hard)
1 lemon, halved
1 cup port
4 cups red wine
3/4 cup sugar
zest of 1 orange

Zabaglione cream
6 egg yolks
6 tablespoons sugar
3/4 cup Malvasia, vin santo, Sauternes, or other sweet wine
1/2 cup heavy cream

To Poach the Pears: Peel the pears, leaving their stems intact. Place each pear immediately into a bowl of ice water with lemon.

Combine the port, red wine, sugar, and orange zest in a large saucepan over medium heat. Add the pears. Bring the liquid to a boil, reduce the heat, and simmer, covered, for about 30 minutes, until the pears are tender. Remove from the heat. Transfer the pears to a platter to cool.

Strain the cooking liquid, removing the orange zest, and return the liquid to the saucepan. Cook over high heat until the liquid reduces to a thin syrupy consistency. Remove from the heat. Spoon the syrup over the pears. Allow it to cool. Then refrigerate the pears, covered.

To Make the Zabaglione: In a nonreactive mixing bowl, whip the egg yolks with the sugar until they are pale yellow and form a ribbon. Slowly beat in the wine and mix thoroughly. Transfer the mixture to a double boiler (or place the mixing bowl over a pot of boiling water), and cook over boiling water, whipping constantly with a whisk until the mixture thickens. It should double in volume and become frothy. Remove from the heat and set the pan in a large bowl of ice water. Continue to whip the zabaglione until it is chilled slightly. Cover the surface of the zabaglione with plastic wrap and refrigerate.

To Serve: Whip the cream until it is stiff. Gently fold the whipped cream into the zabaglione until the mixture is smooth. Place a poached pear on each of 6 dessert plates and add a generous dollop of zabaglione cream.

CAPSOUTO FRÈRES

Winter Menu

NANTUCKET BAY
SCALLOPS WITH
MELTED LEEKS &
BASIL

BRAISED
SWEETBREADS
WITH MADEIRA &
WILD
MUSHROOMS

BLACK MISSION
FIG SOUFFLÉS
WITH WALNUT
CRÈME ANGLAISE

NANTUCKET BAY SCALLOPS WITH MELTED LEEKS & BASIL

THIS RECIPE ALLOWS for eight scallops per person. If Nantucket Bay scallops are not available, choose any fresh bay scallops that are available in early winter. (Do not use the "packed in water" variety.) For this first course, it is essential to warm the plates, keep the leeks warm, and serve immediately. It is also important not to overcook the scallops.

SERVES EIGHT

The leeks
1 bunch leeks, white part only
2 tablespoons clarified butter
1 cup heavy cream
salt
freshly ground pepper

The scallops
15 large basil leaves, washed and dried
64 bay scallops
2 tablespoons clarified butter
1 shallot, finely chopped
1 cup white wine
1 cup heavy cream

To Prepare the Leeks: Trim and quarter the leeks and rinse them thoroughly, separating the layers to get rid of any trapped dirt. Cut them into julienne strips. Drain and dry them. Sweat the leeks (see page 166) with the butter in a saucepan, covered, over low heat, until they are very soft. Remove the cover, raise the heat, and continue cooking until the liquid has almost evaporated. Add the cream and boil, stirring, until it thickens. Remove from the heat. Season with salt and pepper. Set aside.

To Prepare the Scallops and Sauce: Stack the basil leaves and roll them up lengthwise. Slice into a chiffonade (see page 165), and set aside for the garnish.
   Remove the foot from the scallops. Heat the butter in a large sauté pan over medium-high heat until it begins to smoke. Add the scallops and toss. Add the shallots and cook until the scallops are seared. (Do not overcook.)

†WINE SUGGESTION

Jacques Capsouto recommends the following types of French wine to be served with this menu: to accompany the Bay Scallops a Savennières from the Loire Valley. With the Braised Sweetbreads a Marqaux from Bordeaux. And with the Black Mission Fig Soufflés a Sauternes from Bordeaux.

Remove the scallops to a warm plate. Add wine to the pan and reduce the liquid almost completely. Add the cream and reduce until it thickens. Remove from the heat, strain the liquid, and season to taste. Reserve this sauce for the scallops.

To Serve: Place the leeks on warm plates. Top with the scallops, and spoon the sauce over the scallops. Sprinkle slivers of basil chiffonade on top and serve immediately.

CAPSOUTO FRÈRES BRAISED SWEETBREADS WITH MADEIRA & WILD MUSHROOMS

SWEETBREADS ARE A delicacy that go in and out of fashion. Chef Tutino's recipe is fresh and earthy. The wild mushrooms and onions complement the sweetbreads nicely. Begin preparing the sweetbreads one day in advance. It's a good idea to prepare the onions ahead of time, too. The sauce can be prepared up to three days in advance, stored in the refrigerator, and reheated. This reduces the final cooking time before serving to

about 30 minutes. The sauce portion of the recipe calls for mushroom stems; use the stems from the mushroom portion of the recipe. You can also prepare this sauce for braising other meats. Serve this rich entrée with rice, noodles, or orzo.

SERVES EIGHT

The sweetbreads
4 pounds veal sweetbreads
1 cup white vinegar

The sauce
2 tablespoons olive oil
6 cloves garlic, minced
1 onion, coarsely chopped
6 shallots, coarsely chopped
1 carrot, coarsely chopped
2 stalks celery, coarsely chopped
1 cup mushroom stems
4 sprigs fresh thyme
1/4 teaspoon freshly ground pepper
2 cups Madeira
4 cups veal stock

The mushrooms

1/2 pound shiitake mushrooms—washed,
   stemmed, and sliced 1/4-inch thick
1/2 pound oyster mushrooms—washed, and
   sliced 1/4-inch thick
1/2 pound cremini mushrooms—washed,
   stemmed, and sliced 1/4-inch thick
2 tablespoons olive oil
1 tablespoon chopped shallots
salt
freshly ground pepper
1/4 cup brandy
1/2 cup Madeira

The pearl onions

2 baskets pearl onions, peeled
2 tablespoons olive oil
1/2 teaspoon salt
1/2 teaspoon pepper
1/4 teaspoon sugar
2 tablespoons Madeira or port

The assembly

1 cup flour
1 teaspoon salt
1 teaspoon freshly ground pepper
2 tablespoons olive oil
fresh sprigs of parsley and thyme for garnish

To Prepare the Sweetbreads: Soak the sweetbreads in
cold water in a large, nonreactive saucepan for
one hour, changing the water three times. Pour
off the water and add the vinegar. Fill the pan
with cold water to a level of 3 inches above the
sweetbreads. Bring the water to a boil. Then sim-

mer gently for 2 to 5 minutes, until the sweetbreads are just firm. Meanwhile, prepare an ice
bath. Remove the sweetbreads from the simmer-
ing water and immediately plunge them into the
ice bath to cool. Clean the sweetbreads using a
sharp knife to remove any cartilage. Peel off the
outer skin, leaving the fine membrane that holds
the clusters intact. Place the sweetbreads on a
baking dish and cover with waxed paper. Rest a
sheet tray on top. Evenly distribute heavy objects
on the tray to weight it down. Refrigerate the
sweetbreads overnight.

To Make the Sauce: Heat the olive oil in a heavy-
bottomed saucepan over medium heat. Add the
garlic, onions, shallots, carrots, and celery, and
brown the vegetables. Add the mushroom stems,
thyme, and pepper and continue to cook until
the vegetables are crisp. Add the Madeira and
stir to deglaze the pan. Continue cooking until
the mixture reduces by half. Add the stock. (If
you are preparing the sauce ahead of time, stop
at this point, let the sauce cool, and refrigerate it
until about one hour before serving.)

To Prepare the Mushrooms: Heat a large sauté pan until it is very hot, and add the mushrooms, tossing them often until all of the water evaporates. Remove from the heat. Transfer the mushrooms to a dish. Clean the pan and reheat it over high heat. Add the olive oil and the mushrooms and cook until the mushrooms are lightly browned. Add the shallots and season with salt and pepper. Add the brandy and Madeira and continue to cook, stirring, until the liquid evaporates. Remove from the heat. Adjust the seasoning, and set the mushrooms aside.

To Prepare the Pearl Onions: Place the onions in a large saucepan of cold water. Bring the water to a boil. Remove from the heat. Drain the onions and run them under cold water. Brown the onions in olive oil in a sauté pan over medium heat. Add salt, pepper, and sugar. Deglaze the pan with Madeira or port. Serve the onions warm. (If you prepare the onions ahead of time, reheat them with 1/4 cup of stock.)

To Assemble the Entrée: Preheat the oven to 400 degrees. Reheat the sauce in an ovenproof casserole until it comes to a boil. Mix the flour with the salt and pepper in a small bowl. Dust the sweetbreads with this seasoned flour. Heat the olive oil in a sauté pan over medium heat. Sauté the sweetbreads for 2 minutes on each side until they are golden brown. Remove them from the pan and add them to the casserole of sauce. Cover the casserole and bake for 20 minutes.

Remove the casserole from the oven. Take the sweetbreads out of the sauce and set them aside, keeping them warm. Return the sauce to the stove and reduce it by half. Strain it and adjust the seasoning. Add the prepared mushrooms to the sauce and stir.

To Serve: Serve the sweetbreads with the warm mushroom sauce poured over them. Spoon the pearl onions beside the sweetbreads. Garnish with sprigs of parsley and thyme.

CAPSOUTO FRÈRES

BLACK MISSION FIG SOUFFLÉS WITH WALNUT CRÈME ANGLAISE

THESE LIGHT SOUFFLÉS have an exceptional blend of flavors. The preserves, prepared with either fresh or dried figs, can be made in advance and will keep in the refrigerator for up to one month. The Walnut Crème Anglaise can be made one day in advance and chilled until serving time. (When you separate the eggs for the crème anglaise, save the four extra egg whites for the soufflés.) The final preparation happens quickly. Serve these individual soufflés straight from the oven. Each guest can tap the crust of the soufflé open with a spoon and pour in a little of the Walnut Crème Anglaise. Serve with whipped cream if you wish, too.

SERVES EIGHT

The fig preserves

1/2 pound fresh Black Mission figs,
    washed and stemmed*

1/2 cup sugar

1/4 cup red wine

I tablespoon fresh lemon juice

I cinnamon stick

1/2 cup fresh basil, finely chopped

The Walnut Crème Anglaise

3 tablespoons finely chopped walnuts

1/2 cup heavy cream

1/2 cup milk

4 tablespoons sugar

4 egg yolks (from large or extra large
    eggs)

I teaspoon vanilla extract

The soufflés

2 tablespoons plus I teaspoon sugar

2 tablespoons plus I teaspoon brandy

4 egg yolks (from large or extra large eggs)

2 tablespoons fig preserves

8 egg whites (from large or extra large
    eggs)

I teaspoon cream of tartar

2 tablespoons confectioners' sugar

additional confectioners' sugar

*If you are using dried figs instead of fresh
ones, you will need only 1/4 cup of sugar but
3/4 cup of wine. Soak the dried figs (stemmed
and chopped) in the wine for at least 2 hours,
preferably overnight. Use the soaking wine to
cook them.*

To Make the Fig Preserves: Quarter the figs
and combine them with the sugar, wine,
lemon juice, and cinnamon stick in a
saucepan. Bring the liquid to a boil.
Reduce the heat and simmer for 20 minutes, or until the mixture thickens slightly.
Stir in the basil, remove from the heat,
and let the mixture cool. (The preserves
should be slightly thin; if they were too
thick, they would not mix with the soufflé base.)

To Make the Crème Anglaise: Combine the
walnuts with the cream, milk, and 2
tablespoons of sugar in a heavy nonreactive saucepan. Slowly bring the liquid to
a boil and then remove the pan from the
heat. Allow it to cool for 30 minutes.

Return the saucepan to the stove and
bring the liquid to a boil. Meanwhile,
combine the egg yolks and the remaining
2 tablespoons of sugar in a large bowl.
Pour the cream mixture very slowly into
the egg-yolk mixture, whisking constantly.
Pour the mixture back into the saucepan,
and cook it slowly over low heat, stirring
constantly, until the sauce thickens enough
to coat the back of a spoon. Remove from
the heat. Strain the sauce into a bowl that
has been placed in an ice bath. Allow the
custard to cool, and stir in the vanilla
extract. Transfer the custard to a serving
pitcher or bowl and chill it.

To Make the Soufflés: Preheat the oven to 350 degrees. Butter eight 4-ounce ramekins. Dust each one with 1/2 teaspoon of sugar. Sprinkle each with 1/2 teaspoon of brandy.

Combine the egg yolks, the remaining 2 tablespoons of sugar, the remaining 2 tablespoons of brandy, and the 2 tablespoons preserves in a large bowl. Set aside. Beat the egg whites with the cream of tartar in a large metal bowl until the egg whites form soft peaks. Add the confectioners' sugar and continue beating until the peaks are stiff. Fold one-third of the egg-white mixture into the egg-yolk mixture. Then fold the egg-yolk mixture into the egg whites quickly but gently.

Fill each ramekin with soufflé mixture, rounding out the top with a rubber spatula. Place the ramekins on a baking sheet and bake on the center rack of the oven for 15 minutes, or until the soufflés are puffy and golden brown. Remove from the oven.

To Serve: Dust the tops of the soufflés with confectioners' sugar. Serve immediately with the Walnut Crème Anglaise.

CHANTERELLE

Winter Menu

❦

MUSSELS WITH
LIME & BASIL

BEEF WITH BLACK
TRUMPET
MUSHROOMS

WHITE CREAMER
POTATO
PANCAKES WITH
HERBS & GOATS'
MILK CHEESE

FALLEN
CHOCOLATE
SOUFFLÉ CAKE

MUSSELS WITH LIME & BASIL

COMBINING LIME juice and cream requires a leap of faith, but the sauce will not curdle and the taste is very special. You can also make this dish with an assortment of shellfish, such as clams, mussels, oysters, and shrimp.

SERVES SIX

2 pounds mussels,
    washed and bearded
2 tablespoons finely
    chopped shallots
1/2 cup white wine
3 tablespoons lime juice (about 3 limes)
1 cup heavy cream
3 tablespoons unsalted butter
1/4 cup basil leaves, chopped or cut in a fine
    chiffonade (see page 165)
salt

Place the mussels, shallots, and wine in a large nonreactive saucepan with a tight lid. Cover and steam the mussels over high heat until they open. Remove the mussels as they open and keep them warm. Discard any that fail to open.

Strain the liquid into a heavy saucepan and continue cooking it over high heat to reduce it by half. Add the lime juice, cream, and butter, and boil the liquid until it thickens slightly. Add the basil and salt to taste. Adjust the seasoning with lime, salt, or cream if necessary.

To Serve: Place the mussels in 6 warm serving bowls. Pour the sauce over them and serve immediately.

CHANTERELLE   BEEF WITH BLACK TRUMPET MUSHROOMS

FRESH BLACK TRUMPET mushrooms, available during the bleak winter months, impart a rich, earthy flavor to this simple but elegant dish. You may begin by cooking the mushrooms in advance and finish them while the beef is resting. Garnished with seasonal vegetables and served with the White Creamer Potato Pancakes, this special dish comes to the table in less than 30 minutes.

SERVES SIX

† WINE SUGGESTION

World-class sommelier Roger Dagorn has added his suggestions for pairing wines with the recipes that Chef David Waltuck has chosen for this winter menu. To start, serve Tokay Pinot Gris, Vielles Vignes, 1990 from Domaine Zind Humbrecht; for the main course, Côte Rôtie 1988 from Robert Jasmin; and with dessert, Banyuls Rimage 1989 from Parce.

2 tablespoons butter

1 pound fresh black trumpet mushrooms,
　well-cleaned

2 tablespoons olive oil

3 pounds beef fillet

2 tablespoons brandy

1 tablespoon veal or beef *glace* (see page 168)

1 teaspoon fresh lemon juice

1/2 cup heavy cream

salt

freshly ground pepper

Melt 1 tablespoon of the butter in a sauté pan over medium-low heat, and add the mushrooms. Cover and cook the mushrooms until they begin to give off liquid. Remove from the heat and strain the mushrooms, reserving the liquid for the sauce. Set aside.

　Preheat the oven to 400 degrees. Meanwhile, heat the olive oil in a large ovenproof sauté pan over high heat. Sear the beef on all sides to brown it. Remove from the heat. Then roast the beef in the oven for 10 to 15 minutes. (Use a meat thermometer to check for doneness; the meat thermometer will read 120 degrees for rare.) Remove from the oven and place the meat on a carving board. Cover it with a dish towel and let it rest for 10 minutes.

　Meanwhile, résumé cooking the mushrooms. Melt the remaining 1 tablespoon of butter in a sauté pan over high heat. Add the mushrooms and cook them until they are dry and slightly crisped. Remove the pan from the heat and add the brandy. Return the pan to the heat and flame

the brandy. When the flame burns out, add the reserved mushroom liquid, veal or beef *glace*, and lemon juice. Bring the liquid to a boil and add the cream. Continue cooking until the liquid thickens. Remove from the heat. Season with salt, pepper, and additional lemon juice if you wish. Also add any juices from the beef platter.

To Serve: Slice the beef on the bias into 1/4-inch slices and arrange them on 6 warm dinner plates. Spoon the mushroom sauce on top and serve immediately.

CHANTERELLE WHITE CREAMER POTATO PANCAKES WITH HERBS & GOATS' MILK CHEESE

THESE DELICATE POTATO pancakes resemble crêpes more than traditional potato latkes. They have a light but complex flavor. The batter must be made at least one hour in advance and can be made up to six hours in advance and stored in the refrigerator. To time this dish with the Beef with Black Trumpet Mushrooms, cook the potato pancakes while the beef is in the oven.

SERVES SIX

1 pound white creamer or fingerling potatoes,
   peeled
1/4 cup milk
2 tablespoons fresh goats' milk cheese
3 whole eggs
3 egg whites
1 tablespoon heavy cream
1 tablespoon finely chopped fresh herbs, such as
   parsley, chives, chervil, or tarragon
pinch of salt
pinch of freshly ground pepper
1 cup olive oil or clarified butter, or a combination of both

---

Place the potatoes in a pot of salted water, bring
to a boil and cook until the potatoes are soft.
Remove from the heat. Pour the water off the
potatoes, add the milk and cheese, and mash well.
Pass the mixture through a food mill into a large
bowl. Stir in the eggs and egg whites. Then stir in
the cream. Add the herbs, salt, and pepper. Cover
the batter with plastic wrap and refrigerate at least
1 hour.

    Pour the oil or butter into a heavy skillet to a
depth of 1/2 inch. Heat it at a medium-high temperature. Drop large spoonfuls of batter into the
hot oil and cook until air holes appear around the
edges of the pancakes. Flip them over and cook
until both sides are light brown. Transfer the pancakes to a paper-towel-covered plate. Continue
cooking the pancakes in batches, adding oil or
butter as necessary. Serve immediately. (Or keep
them in a warm oven for up to 20 minutes.)

CHANTERELLE · FALLEN CHOCOLATE SOUFFLÉ CAKE

THIS SENSATIONAL CHOCOLATE
dessert is easy to prepare but must be made a
day in advance. When you cut the cake, be sure
to run the knife under hot water and wipe the
knife clean between cuts.

MAKES ONE 9-INCH CAKE

---

1 pound semisweet chocolate
1 cup sweet butter
9 eggs, separated
1/2 cup plus 1 teaspoon sugar
3 tablespoons cocoa powder
3 tablespoons confectioners' sugar
1/2 pint heavy cream, whipped

Preheat the oven to 300 degrees. Butter and flour a 9-inch springform pan. Line the bottom with parchment paper. Then butter and flour the lining.

Melt the chocolate and butter in a double boiler over low heat, stirring to blend. Remove from the heat and set aside to cool. In a large mixing bowl, beat the egg yolks with 1/2 cup of sugar until the mixture forms a ribbon. In a separate bowl, combine the egg whites with 1 teaspoon of sugar and beat until the mixture forms soft peaks. Set aside.

In a separate bowl, fold together one-third of the chocolate mixture with one-third of the egg-yolk mixture. Then fold in one-third of the egg whites. Repeat until the three mixtures are incorporated. Pour the batter into the prepared pan and bake for 30 minutes. (Do not overbake. The center of the cake should still be soft.) Remove

from the oven and place on a wire rack to cool for 3 hours.

Dust the top of the cake with 1 tablespoon of the cocoa, sifted. Then dust it with 1 tablespoon of the confectioners' sugar, sifted. Then repeat. Refrigerate the cake overnight in the pan. Before serving, let the cake stand at room temperature for 1 hour. Dust it again with the remaining 1 tablespoon each of cocoa and confectioners' sugar, and remove the cake from the pan.

To Serve: Slice the cake with a hot knife and serve it with whipped cream.

NOSMO KING

Winter Menu

ROASTED
SOURDOUGH
BREAD WITH
GOATS' MILK
CHEESE, RED
PEPPERS, BASIL &
BLACK OLIVE
TAPENADE

SEARED TUNA
WITH SPINACH,
WHITE BEANS &
LIME-MARJORAM
VINAIGRETTE

STEAMED
CRANBERRY
PUDDING

ROASTED SOURDOUGH BREAD WITH GOATS' MILK CHEESE, RED PEPPERS, BASIL & BLACK OLIVE TAPENADE

PURCHASE A MEDIUM-sized round loaf of sourdough bread for this recipe. The tapenade can be made one or two days in advance and kept in a covered dish in the refrigerator. All of the ingredients should be at room temperature before assembling them. The quality of the tapenade will largely depend on the quality of olives. Choose imported black olives such as Alfonse or Kalamata. For a colorful tray of hors d'oeuvres consider scaling this dish down by using a sourdough baguette cut into 1/4-inch slices.

SERVES FOUR

The tapenade
1/2 cup cured olives, pitted
2 teaspoons fresh lemon zest
1 tablespoon fresh lemon juice
1 tablespoon coarsely chopped Italian parsley

The assembly
1 cup fresh goats' milk cheese at room temperature
pinch of salt
pinch of pepper
4 1/2-inch slices sourdough bread
1/2 cup olive oil
1 cup basil leaves
2 red bell peppers—roasted, halved, and seeded
4 cups assorted salad greens, washed and dried

To Make the Tapenade: Coarsely blend the olives, lemon zest, juice, and parsley in a food processor or blender. Set aside.

To Assemble the Appetizer: Using a fork, combine the cheese with the salt and pepper in a small bowl, and set it aside.

Preheat the oven to 350 degrees. Brush each side of the sourdough bread lightly with a little olive oil. Place the bread on a baking sheet and

†WINE SUGGESTION

Chef Alan Harding recommends Chesterfield Ale from Yuengling Brewery in Pennsylvania to accompany the appetizer, followed by Gristina Cabernet Franc from Norfolk, Long Island to accompany the main course.

toast it in the oven. (Watch carefully to make sure the bread does not burn.)

Remove from the oven and immediately spread the cheese uniformly on each slice. Top the cheese with the basil leaves, covering it completely. Top the basil with the roasted pepper. Cut each piece of bread into quarters with a serrated knife and top each with a dollop of tapenade.

To Serve: Distribute the salad greens among 4 salad plates. Drizzle the remaining olive oil over the greens, and top with the quarters of bread. Serve immediately.

NOSMO KING | SEARED TUNA WITH SPINACH, WHITE BEANS & LIME-MARJORAM VINAIGRETTE

THIS IS A great dish to serve guests who have a reputation for being late. All of the ingredients can be ready for final preparation, which takes only minutes. Chef Harding recommends serving this tuna very rare. Ask the fishmonger for 24 ounces of yellowfin tuna to be cut into equal blocks. If yellowfin is not available, substitute any fresh tuna. If you are using tuna steaks, cut them into three-inch cubes. These pieces will cook quickly. Prepare the beans beforehand, if possible. Or use canned beans—white kidney beans (cannellini) or Great Northern beans.

SERVES FOUR

The vinaigrette
2 tablespoons fresh lime juice
2 tablespoons fresh marjoram, chopped
4 tablespoons olive oil

The tuna, spinach, and beans
4 to 6 tablespoons coarsely ground black pepper
24 ounces yellowfin tuna, cut into 4 equal blocks
2 tablespoons plus 1 teaspoon olive oil
2 tablespoons canola oil
2 pounds fresh spinach, thoroughly cleaned with tough stems removed
1 cup fully cooked white beans, drained
pinch of salt
pinch of freshly ground pepper

To Make the Vinaigrette: Whisk together the lime juice and marjoram. Continue to whisk while you add the olive oil, one tablespoon at a time. Set aside.

NOSMO KING
RESTAURANT BAR CATERING
54 VARICK STREET NYC 10013
212 966 1239, FAX 212 966 1714

To Prepare the Tuna: Place the coarsely ground pepper on a plate. Lightly coat the tuna pieces on both sides with pepper. Heat 2 tablespoons of the olive oil with the canola oil in a heavy skillet until hot, but not smoking. Sear the tuna evenly on both sides. Remove from the heat and keep the tuna warm.

To Prepare the Spinach and Beans: Heat the remaining 1 teaspoon of olive oil in a large skillet, and sauté the spinach over medium heat until it is wilted. Add the beans and season with salt and pepper. Continue to cook, stirring gently, for 5 minutes, until the spinach is done and the beans are warm.

To Serve: Divide the spinach mixture evenly among 4 warm dinner plates. Cut each large piece of tuna into 3 pieces and arrange them on top of the spinach and beans. Drizzle the vinaigrette over the tuna, beans, and spinach, and serve immediately.

STEAMED CRANBERRY PUDDING

THIS PUDDING IS steamed in a 46-ounce can, the type used for tomato juice. Remove the top from one end of the can. Trim the sharp edges, and clean the can thoroughly. The pudding must steam for at least 1 1/2 hours and is best served warm. Cook it while your guests are dining, so they can enjoy the spicy aroma that will fill the house. Serve the pudding warm with vanilla ice cream or whipped cream.

MAKES ONE PUDDING

3/4 cup whole wheat flour
1/2 cup all-purpose flour
1 teaspoon baking soda
1 teaspoon cinnamon
1/2 teaspoon salt
1/4 teaspoon ground cloves
1/2 cup fresh orange juice
1/2 cup honey
2 cups chopped cranberries
1/2 cup chopped walnuts
2 tablespoons orange zest
Vanilla ice cream or whipped cream

Oil the inside of a 46-ounce can with vegetable oil, and line the bottom and sides with parchment paper or waxed paper. Oil the lining in the can. Place a rack in the bottom of a large stockpot (or use a canning kettle with a rack insert).

In a large mixing bowl, combine the whole wheat flour, all-purpose flour, baking soda, cinnamon, salt, and cloves. Stir to blend well. Add the orange juice and honey, and stir to mix well. Add the cranberries,

walnuts, and zest, and stir to combine.

Spoon the batter into the prepared can and spread it smooth. Cover the opening tightly with aluminum foil. Tap the can several times on the counter to distribute the batter. Tie the foil tightly to the can using kitchen twine. Rest the can on the rack in the stockpot. Fill the pot with water to a level halfway up the can. Place the lid on the stockpot and bring the water to a boil over high heat. Lower the heat to medium and steam the pudding for 1 1/2 hours, adding water to the pot as necessary. Lift the can from the pot and allow the pudding to cool slightly before you unmold it.

To Serve: Slice the pudding into 1/2-inch-thick rounds and serve immediately with vanilla ice cream or whipped cream.

The TRIBECA

COOKBOOK

THE ODEON

Winter Menu
❦

PAN ROAST OF
OYSTERS WITH
POBLANO CHILES
ON TOASTED
CORNBREAD

GRILLED LAMB
SHANKS WITH
PRESERVED
LEMONS ON
ARUGULA

PEAR
TURNOVERS

PAN ROAST OF OYSTERS WITH POBLANO CHILES ON TOASTED CORNBREAD

THE BLEND AND balance of flavors in this dish is joyful. The cornbread can be baked one day in advance and toasted when ready to serve. You can do the last-minute cooking as someone opens and pours the wine. When you purchase the oysters, ask the fishmonger to open them and reserve the liquid for you.

SERVES SIX

The cornbread
1 cup cornmeal
1 cup flour
1/2 cup sugar
2 1/2 teaspoons baking powder
1/2 teaspoon salt
1/4 teaspoon freshly ground pepper
6 tablespoons butter, softened to room temperature
1/8 cup honey

✝WINE SUGGESTION

Chef Stephen Lyle recommends serving an Oak Knoll 1991 Pinot Noir with this meal.

2 eggs, lightly beaten
1 cup milk

The oysters
6 tablespoons butter
36 plump East Coast oysters, shucked and drained
liquid from oysters
1/2 cup poblano chiles—roasted, finely seeded, peeled, and diced
3 tablespoons crème fraîche
3 tablespoons fresh lime juice
4 tablespoons chopped cilantro
dash of Tabasco sauce
whole cilantro leaves for garnish

To Prepare the Cornbread: Preheat the oven to 350 degrees. Lightly grease an 8-inch square pan.

Combine the cornmeal, flour, sugar, baking powder, salt, and pepper in a large mixing bowl. Add the butter and combine the ingredients with your fingers until the mixture resembles coarse meal. Form a well in the center and add the honey, eggs, and milk. Blend the mixture quickly with a fork. Pour it into the prepared pan and bake for 30 minutes, or until a knife inserted in the center comes out clean. Remove from the oven and let it cool.

To Prepare the Oysters and Serve: Preheat the broiler. Cut the cornbread into 6 equal rectangles. Split each one in half, lightly toast it under the broiler, and place it in a soup plate.

Heat a sauté pan over medium-low heat and add the butter. Heat it until it becomes foamy. Then add the oysters and cook them about 2 minutes, until the edges begin to curl. (Halfway through the cooking time, gently turn them once.) Remove the oysters with a slotted spoon and place them on the cornbread. Set aside and keep warm.

Add the reserved oyster liquid and chiles to the sauté pan and cook until the sauce begins to

thicken. Add the crème fraîche and reduce the sauce until it is thick. Remove from the heat. Stir in the lime juice, chopped cilantro, and Tabasco sauce. Adjust the seasoing to taste and pour the sauce over the oysters. Garnish with whole cilantro leaves and serve immediately.

THE ODEON — GRILLED LAMB SHANKS WITH PRESERVED LEMONS ON ARUGULA

CHEF LYLE CALLS this recipe "barbecue for cave people, not for the faint of heart." The preserved lemons must be made two weeks in advance, but they will keep in the refrigerator for at least a month. (A recipe for preserved lemons is provided in the Basics and Techniques section of this book, page 165.) The lamb shanks are marinated overnight. They can be baked in advance and refrigerated for up to three days. Then you can grill or broil them just before serving. Make the condiment at least two hours before serving to ensure the intensity of its flavor.

SERVES SIX

The lamb

I bunch fresh thyme

I whole head garlic, peeled and lightly crushed

I small bunch fresh oregano or marjoram, chopped

I teaspoon cracked black pepper

I preserved lemon, chopped (see page 165)

I cup olive oil

l onion, chopped

2 carrots, chopped

3 stalks celery, chopped

6 lamb shanks

salt

The condiment

I roasted red bell pepper—peeled, seeded, and diced small (see page 166)

I preserved lemon, finely diced (see page 165)

1/2 small red onion, diced small

1/4 cup oil-cured or Niçoise olives, pitted and coarsely chopped

2 tablespoons fresh lemon juice

I tablespoon chopped Italian parsley

I tablespoon chopped mint

I teaspoon ground cumin

The arugula

3 tablespoons olive oil

1 tablespoon fresh lemon juice

salt

freshly ground pepper

6 handfuls arugula (2 bunches)—washed, dried, and stemmed

6 wedges fresh lemon for garnish

To Marinate the Lamb Shanks: Pick the leaves from the bunch of thyme. Reserve the stems to toss on the grill. Then chop the leaves lightly and place them in a deep baking dish. Add the garlic, oregano or marjoram, cracked pepper, preserved lemon, olive oil, onions, carrots, and celery. Place the lamb shanks in this marinade. Cover and refrigerate overnight. (Turn the meat once or twice.)

To Cook the Lamb Shanks: Remove the lamb shanks from the baking dish and scrape most of the marinade off. (Reserve the marinade.) Preheat the oven to 325 degrees. Meanwhile, salt the lamb shanks and sear them in a large, heavy saucepan over a high heat, browning on all sides. Remove from the heat. Transfer the shanks and reserved marinade to a large casserole with a tight-fitting lid. Bake for 3 hours, or until the meat falls off the bone and is very tender. (Turn the shanks once or twice. Do not let the marinade burn.)

Remove the shanks from the oven and let them cool in the casserole. Sprinkle any pan juices over the shanks. Set aside. (If you are preparing the lamb shanks in advance, transfer them to a large plate, cover, and refrigerate them at this time. Let them sit at room temperature for an hour before you grill them.)

To Prepare the Condiment: Combine all of the condiment ingredients in a medium-sized bowl and leave at room temperature for at least 2 hours, stirring occasionally. Adjust the seasoning before serving.

To Serve: Prepare the grill or broiler. Grill or broil the shanks until they are hot and lightly charred on the outside. Meanwhile, prepare the arugula: combine the olive oil, lemon juice, salt, and pepper in a small bowl; pour over the arugula and toss gently. Divide the dressed arugula among 6 plates. Place one on each bed of arugula, and garnish with equal portions of condiment and a wedge of lemon. Serve immediately.

THE ODEON

PEAR TURNOVERS

THIS IS A very rewarding dessert to make, combining ease of preparation with beautiful and delicious results. Chef Lyle serves these turnovers warm, with vanilla ice cream. Because puff pastry is always best as it comes out of the oven, prepare the turnovers ahead of time and keep them in the freezer until just before baking. You can store the unbaked turnovers in the freezer for up to one month in an airtight container.

SERVES SIX

1 package frozen puff pastry sheets
3 to 4 Bartlett or Anjou pears
1/4 cup apricot preserves
2 tablespoons cornstarch
1/8 teaspoon cinnamon
2 tablespoons almond paste
1 egg plus one egg yolk
1 tablespoon confectioners' sugar for dusting

Remove the puff pastry from the freezer 20 minutes before rolling it out.

Peel the pears and dice them into 1/2-inch pieces. (If the pears are hard, dice them smaller.) You will need about 2 cups of pears. Combine them in a mixing bowl with the preserves, cornstarch, and cinnamon. Set aside.

Roll out the pastry sheet to about 12 x 18 inches, and cut out six 6-inch squares. (Refreeze or discard any leftover pastry.) Crumble one-sixth of the almond paste into the center of each square. Distribute the pear mixture among the 6 squares. Fold the dough over the filling to form a triangle. Crimp the edges with a fork. Place the turnovers on a baking sheet. Place in the freezer for at least 1 hour before baking. (If planning to store for longer, transfer to an airtight container once the turnovers are firm.)

Preheat the oven to 400 degrees. Whisk the whole egg and the egg yolk together in a small bowl. Brush the egg mixture over each turnover, and cut a small slit in the top of it. Bake the turnovers for 10 to 15 minutes, or until they are puffy and golden brown. Remove from the oven and allow the turnovers to cool slightly. Dust them with confectioners' sugar and serve warm.

BASICS AND TECHNIQUES

THIS SECTION EXPLAINS and expands upon some of the cooking methods used throughout the cookbook. It also includes several stock recipes, which are useful for stews and sauces as well as soups. Use this section as a reference guide.

CHIFFONADE

This term describes the process and the end product of finely slicing fresh leafy herbs or greens, usually for garnish. To chiffonnade fresh basil leaves, for example, stack the leaves and roll them tightly. Then slice through the roll crosswise with a sharp knife to make fine slivers of basil.

CLARIFIED BUTTER

Clarified butter is butter from which all of the milk solids have been removed. It has a higher burning point than regular butter. To clarify butter, put it in a heavy saucepan and melt it over a very low heat. At first, the milk solids will rise to the top. But as the butter continues to cook, the solids will sink to the bottom of the pan. You can then skim off the pure yellow clarified butter on top. Or you can separate out the milk solids by pouring the melted butter through a fine-mesh strainer lined with a paper towel. Discard the white deposit left in the pan, as well as what you capture in the strainer.

CRÈME FRAÎCHE

To make your own crème fraîche, whisk together 2 cups of heavy cream with 5 tablespoons of buttermilk. Pour the mixture into a jar, shake well, and cover. Place it in a warm spot for 12 hours, until the cream has thickened. Refrigerate it for up to one week.

CRACKED PEPPER

Wrap whole peppercorns in a dish towel and gently pound them with a heavy object, such as a rolling pin, to partially crush and crack them. Use cracked pepper in salads, soups, and marinades.

DRIED BEANS

Rinse dried beans several times and check them for stones or grit before soaking them. Most dried beans may be soaked in cold water for 6 to 8 hours in a large bowl or saucepan. Fill the pan to a level of 2 inches above the beans. Then drain the beans, rinse them, and cook them according to the recipe. A quick method for soaking beans is to place them in a pot of cold water, cover the pot, bring the water to a boil, and let it boil for 2 minutes. Remove the pot from the heat and let the beans stand in the covered pot for 1 hour. You may use either the long-soak method or the quick-soak method before proceeding with any of the bean recipes in this book.

PRESERVED LEMONS

3 lemons
3 tablespoons kosher salt
olive oil

Scrub the skin of the lemons clean and remove the small green stem residue. Quarter the lemons, stopping the cuts about one-half inch from the bottom. Spread the wedges and pour salt into the center. Gently squeeze the lemons shut, tightly pack them in a plastic container, and refrigerate them. Gently shake the container every two days, but do not drain it. After two weeks, transfer the lemons to a glass jar. Pour the residual juice over the lemons and top with olive oil to cover the lemons.

Store in the refrigerator. Preserved lemons will keep for months.

ROASTING GARLIC

Preheat the oven to 325 degrees. You can roast any number of heads of garlic at once. Remove some of the excess outer peels from the garlic, but keep each head intact. Place the heads on a large piece of aluminum foil, and drizzle olive oil over them. Close up the foil and roast the garlic in the oven for about 1 hour, until the garlic is soft.

ROASTING PEPPERS

Select firm peppers. Wash them and pat them dry. Preheat the broiler. Place the peppers, lying on their sides, on a baking sheet or roasting pan. Broil the peppers until the skins are charred on all sides, including the tops and bottoms. (You also can roast peppers on the stove. Set the peppers directly in the flame of a gas burner, and turn them so they char evenly all over.) Remove the peppers from the oven and immediately place them in a brown paper bag or any covered container. Close the bag and let the peppers steam. Remove one pepper from the bag and cut it in half. Remove and discard the stem and seeds. Peel away the charred skin or rinse under running water. Repeat with the other peppers in the bag. or any covered container (Reseal the bag each time so

the peppers stay warm.) Place the peppers in a jar and cover them with olive oil. Stored in the refrigerator, the roasted peppers will keep for one week.

SWEATING VEGETABLES

Vegetables, when cooked slowly in a bit of oil or fat, covered, over low heat, will give up some of their liquid to the pot. This process is called sweating. Sweating vegetables is often the first step when making soups or sauces. The liquid produced in this way allows the flavors of the vegetables and any other seasoning you add to them to completely permeate the sauce.

WARMED PLATES

At fine restaurants, waiters repeat the phrase "The plate is hot!" with each hot entrée they serve to patrons—and for good reason. No chef wants to disappoint a client with a lukewarm meal or be asked to reheat an entrée that has been prepared to perfection. Nor would many dinner guests in your home be so rude as to mention that the meal is cold. Therefore, it is always a good idea to warm the plates of any dish to be served warm. Just place the plates in a warm oven for a few minutes before serving, to ensure the perfection of temperature.

WATER BATH

A water bath, or bain-marie, is used when baking custards. The hot water insulates the eggs and keeps them from curdling. To make a water bath, select a deep pan that is larger than the baking dish in which the custard is baked. Or select a deep pan that will hold all of the ramekins. Place the ramekins or custard baking dish in the larger pan. Fill the larger pan with water and place it in the oven.

Soup Stocks

CHICKEN STOCK

This basic recipe yields about 3 quarts of rich and flavorful stock.

---

1 large chicken (4 to 6 pounds), cut up, plus any
   miscellaneous chicken bones or parts such as
   wings, necks, or backs
2 stalks celery, with leaves
2 carrots
1 leek
1 parsnip
1 onion studded with 2 cloves
stems from 1/4 bunch parsley
1 tablespoon whole peppercorns
1 bay leaf
1 sprig thyme
1/2 head garlic, left intact

Place the chicken in a stockpot and cover it with water, and bring the liquid to a boil. Skim the surface to remove the foam. Then add the vegetables and remaining ingredients. Lower the heat to a simmer. (You should see an occasional bubble rise to the surface.) Cook at this temperature for 3 to 6 hours, skimming as necessary. Remove from the heat. Strain the stock through a colander into a large bowl and discard the bones and vegetables. Strain the stock again through a fine-mesh sieve lined with cheesecloth. Chill the stock. Remove the fat from the liquid, and freeze or refrigerate the stock. It will keep in the refrigerator for several days, but you should boil it for a few minutes every 3 days.

BEEF STOCK

This basic recipe yields about 3 to 5 quarts.

---

4 pounds beef bones or beef and veal bones, cracked
2 to 3 pounds mixed meat scraps or shinbeef
2 carrots
2 stalks celery
2 onions, studded with 2 cloves
2 leeks
1 sprig thyme
1 bay leaf
6 sprigs parsley
1/2 head garlic
1 tablespoon whole peppercorns

Place the bones in the stockpot and cover them by at least 3 inches of cold water. Place the stockpot over a high heat and bring the liquid to a boil. Skim the foam from the top of the liquid until it no longer accumulates, about 5 minutes. Add all remaining ingredients and more water, if necessary, to keep the ingredients covered by 2 to 3 inches. Skim as necessary and let the water return to a boil. Reduce the heat to a low simmer, and cook for 4 to 6 hours, skimming as necessary. Remove from the heat. Strain the stock carefully through a colander into a large bowl and discard the bones and vegetables. Strain the stock again through a fine-mesh sieve lined with a cheesecloth. Chill the stock. Remove the fat from the liquid, and freeze or refrigerate the stock. It will keep in the refrigerator for several days, but you should boil it for a few minutes every 3 days.

VEAL STOCK

Veal and veal bones produce a lot of residue when cooked. Therefore, it is best to blanch them for 5 minutes first and rinse them under cold water. Make Veal Stock according to the recipe for Beef Stock. Use 4 pounds of cracked veal bones and 2 to 3 pounds of veal scraps. Yields about 3 to 5 quarts.

VEAL OR BEEF *GLACE*

Three quarts of stock will reduce to about 1 cup of *glace.* Strain the veal or beef stock and make sure it is thoroughly degreased. (This is best done by chilling it so all of the fat rises to the top and solidifies. Then you can easily lift the fat off. Remove any lingering bits by blotting paper towel on the surface.) Boil the stock in a large saucepan or stockpot until it reduces to about 1 quart. Strain it through a sieve and transfer it to a smaller saucepan. Continue to boil it down, making sure it doesn't burn. Reduce it to a thick, syrupy consistency. Strain it once again and let it cool. Refrigerate or freeze the *glace.* (Freeze it in ice cube trays for easy dispensing.)

FISH STOCK

This basic recipe yields 2 to 3 quarts of a rich and flavorful stock. Choose scraps from any non-oily fish (not salmon, bluefish, or mackerel). You may also use shrimp, lobster, or crab shells.

---

3 to 4 pounds fish heads, bones, and trimmings
1 cup white wine (or more)
1 onion, sliced
1 leek, cleaned and coarsely chopped
1/4 bunch parsley
1 bay leaf
1 sprig thyme
juice of 1 lemon

Place the fish scraps in a stockpot and cover them with wine and water. Bring the liquid to a boil and add the remaining ingredients. Lower the heat and simmer for 30 minutes. Strain the stock through a colander into a large bowl and discard the bones and vegetables. Strain it again through a fine-mesh sieve lined with cheesecloth or paper towel. Chill the stock. Remove the fat from the liquid, and freeze or refrigerate the stock. It will keep in the refrigerator for several days, but you should boil it for a few minutes every 3 days.

The
TRIBECA

COOKBOOK

SOURCES GUIDE

ALL OF THE chefs featured in this cookbook
use the finest fresh ingredients to prepare their
dishes. We offer the following sources for fresh
ingredients, in case your local markets cannot
provide them. In keeping with the scope of the
book, we begin with TriBeCa distributors, followed by distributors that carry a wide range of
products, followed by distributors that carry spe-
cific products (herbs and spices, meat and poultry, and so on). Most of these suppliers offer
next-day shipping.

DISTRIBUTORS IN TRIBECA

AUX DELICES DES BOIS
4 Leonard Street
New York, NY 10013
(800) 666-1232
Call to get a catalog, which includes all varieties
of mushrooms, truffles, herbs, Mesclun, and
huitlacoche.

A. L. BAZZINI COMPANY, INC.
339 Greenwich Street
New York, NY 10013
(800) 228-0172
Bazzini has been located in TriBeCa since 1886.
On any given day, the corner of Greenwich and
Jay streets is full of the aroma of roasting nuts.
Bazzini's catalog features oils, grains, beans, dried
fruit, and candy, as well as nuts. The catalog is
designed for the holiday season, but the retail
store will ship items year-round.

GENERAL INGREDIENT DISTRIBUTORS

The following companies offer a wide range of
items, all listed in their catalogs. When in doubt,
call their 800 numbers and ask if they have the
product you need.

DEAN AND DELUCA
560 Broadway
New York, NY 10012
(800) 221-7714
Located just a few blocks north of TriBeCa in
Soho, Dean and DeLuca holds its own as one of
this country's finest food stores. Its catalog offers
fine oils, vinegars, pastas, dried herbs, dried black
mission figs, and fresh ones in season.

BALDUCCI'S
42–25 12th Street
Long Island City, NY 11101
(800) 225-3822
This New York City establishment offers the
freshest and the finest, all of which is featured in
its catalog: meat, fish, poultry, pasta, cheeses, prepared desserts, coffees and teas, and other specialty
gourmet items. The catalog costs $5, but this cost
is applied toward your initial purchase.

FRIEDA'S
4465 Corporate Center Drive
Los Alamitos, CA 90720-2561
(800) 241-1771
In addition to a catalog that features wonderful
gift baskets, Frieda's has a product list of over 350

items, including many types of fresh and dried fruits and vegetables and spices. Be sure to request both the catalog and the product list for a complete understanding of Frieda's offerings.

HERBS AND SPICES

AUX DELICES DES BOIS
See above, page 169.

FOX HILL FARM
444 W. Michigan Avenue
Parma, MI 49269
(517) 531-3179
For over 15 years, Fox Hill Farm has been supplying restaurants and individuals with herb plants and freshly cut herbs. Its catalog includes several varieties of thyme and oregano, rosemary, sage, cilantro, mint, tarragon, epazote, watercress, and arugula—all available year-round.

FOODS OF ALL NATIONS
2121 Ivy Road
Charlottesville, VA 22903
(800) 368-3998
For unusual and international ingredients, contact Foods of All Nations. Check the company's catalog for epazote, achiote paste, and other hard-to-find items.

THE SPICE GOURMET
Route 1, 150–A
Java, VA 24565
(800) 952-8783
This company offers all types of dried herbs, including saffron. The Spice Gourmet also can supply vanilla beans and many varieties of peppers, including ancho.

THE SPICE MERCHANT
P.O. Box 524
Jackson Hole, WY 83001
(800) 551-5999
Look to the Spice Merchant catalog for special spices used in cooking Thai, Indonesian, Chinese, or Japanese foods.

TOMMY TANG'S THAI SEASONINGS
P. O. Box 46700
Los Angeles, CA 90046
(213) 874-3883
For a number of years, Tommy Tang's restaurant was located on Greenwich Street in TriBeCa. His Thai seasonings and sauces are readily available in gourmet stores. You can also contact Tommy Tang's directly to have ingredients shipped to your home.

MEAT AND POULTRY

D' ARTAGNAN
399–419 St. Paul Avenue
Jersey City, NJ 07306
(800) 327-8246
D'Artagnan's catalog includes foie gras, duck breasts, chicken, turkey, quail, squab, rabbit, and prosciutto. The company does not carry veal or beef.

DEER VALLEY FARM
R. D. 1
Guilford, NY 13780
(607) 764-8556
Located in Shenango County, New York, Deer Valley Farm offers organic chicken, beef, pork, and veal, all of which can be shipped UPS. Ask for the farm's catalog.

SIGNATURE PRIME MEATS
P.O. Box 128
North Aurora, IL 60542
(800) 621-0397
Signature's catalog offers an extensive line of gourmet meats, including all cuts of beef, lamb, pork, and veal.

DAIRY PRODUCTS

IDEAL CHEESE
1205 2nd Avenue
New York, NY 10021
(800) 382-0109
The $2 cost of a catalog from Ideal Cheese will be applied toward the initial purchase. Ideal will ship a large variety of dairy products, including sheep's milk yogurt, *robiola*, and crème fraîche.

MOZZARELLA COMPANY
2944 Elm Street
Dallas, TX 75226
(800) 798-2954
The Mozzarella Company carries more than mozzarella. Its catalog offers Crème fraîche, mascarpone, many types of goats' milk cheese, including goats' milk ricotta, and other finds.

DRIED BEANS AND GRAINS

BESS' BEANS
P.O. Box 1542
Charleston, S.C. 29402
(800) 233-2326
This company offers ordinary and extraordinary beans for cooking and eating enjoyment.

WALNUT ACRES
Penn's Creek, PA 17862
(800) 433-3998
The Walnut Acres catalog has a vast variety of dried beans and fruits, including black mission dried figs. This company also carries an extensive line of flours, fresh produce, cereals, pancake mixes, and syrups. All of its products are organically produced.

DRIED FRUITS AND VEGETABLES

AMERICAN SPOON FOODS
1668 Clarion Avenue
Petoskey, MI 49770
(800) 222-5886
American Spoon is quickly becoming a well-known label in specialty food stores for dried fruits—including cherries, cranberries, strawberries, blueberries, pears, and persimmons. It also carries jams, sugarless spoon fruits, and other fruit products.

A. L. BAZZINI COMPANY, INC.
See above, page 169.

L'ESPRIT DE CAMPAGNE
P. O. Box 3130
Winchester, VA 22604
(703) 955-1014
L'Esprit de Campagne is dedicated to producing high quality, sulphur-free dried tomatoes and fruits. All products are certified kosher.

FISH

CAVIARTERIA
502 Park Avenue
New York, NY 10022
(800) 422-8427
This company's catalog offers a wide selection of fish products, including many varieties of smoked salmon, caviar, Dungeness crabmeat, kippers, clams, and shad roe.

DUCKTRAP RIVER FISH FARM
R.R. 2, Box 378
Lincolnville, ME 04849
(800) 828-3825
Directly from Maine comes smoked salmon, trout, mussels, scallops, and shrimp.

FALMOUTH FISH MARKET
157 Tea Ticket Highway
East Falmouth, MA 02536
(800) 628-0045
This Massachusetts market is one of the few mail-order sources that we could find for striped bass. The market offers an extensive variety of the freshest seafood products.

HEGG & HEGG
801 Marine Drive
Port Angeles, WA 98362
(800) 435-3474
This company ships a large selection of shellfish and other products fresh from the Pacific Northwest.

FRESH FRUITS AND VEGETABLES

DIAMOND ORGANICS
P. O. Box 2159
Freedom, CA 95019
(800) 922-2396
This company offers organic products from the largest organic growing area in the world. Its catalog offers an extensive line of fresh greens, including fiddlehead ferns, fresh fava beans, and baby lettuces; fresh mushrooms, including shiitakes, chanterelles, and oysters; many varieties of peaches, plums, quince, apples, and pears; many exotic dried fruits, such as persimmons, kiwifruits, mangoes, tomatoes, pineapples, and cherries; and nuts, such as almonds, walnuts, chestnuts, and pistachios.

FRIEDA'S
See above, page 169.

INDEX

Achiote Paste, 80
Apples
    Apple Tart, 138–39
    Warm Apple Empanadas with Orange Hibiscus Sauce, 121–22
Arqua, 14, 64–67, 134–39
Arroz Verde, 83
Asparagus
    Asparagus, Morels, Ramps and Fiddlehead Ferns with Orange
        Oil and Edible Flowers, 36–37
    Asparagus with Horseradish Vinaigrette and Pickled Beets,
        43–44
    Fresh Fava Bean and Asparagus Soup, 90
Avocado Sauce, 81–82
Ayoubi, Khalil, 21

Barocco, 14–15, 24–29, 140–43
Beans
    cooking, 165
    Fresh Fava Bean and Asparagus Soup, 90
    Pan-Fried Soft-Shell Crabs with Tomato Vinaigrette and Fava
        Beans with Shallots and Summer Savory, 44–46
    Pasta Fagioli, 134–35
    Seared Tuna with Spinach, White Beans and Lime-Marjoram
        Vinaigrette, 157–58
    Tostadas de Camarónes, 78–79
    Warm Shrimp and Bean Salad, 24–26
    Whipped White Beans, 115
Beef
    Beef *Glace*, 168
    Beef Stock, 167
    Beef with Black Trumpet Mushrooms, 151–153
    Yucatán Grilled Steak, Chicken Breasts and Whole Red
        Snapper, 80
Beets
    Asparagus with Horseradish Vinaigrette and Pickled Beets,
        43–44
    Warm Goats' Milk Cheese in Phyllo with Roasted Beets,
        112–13
Biscotti, Almond, 76–77
Black Mission Fig Soufflés with Walnut Crème Anglaise, 148–50
Blom, David, 18–19, 126
Blue Potatoes with Crème Fraîche and Caviar, 109–10
Bread
    Olive Breadsticks, 40
    Panzanella with Mixed Field Greens, 73–74
    Roasted Sourdough Bread with Goats' Milk Cheese, Red
        Peppers, Basil and Black Olive Tapenade, 156–57
    Spiced Spoonbread, 94
    Strawberry Bread Pudding, 42
Butter, clarified, 165

Cakes
    Chocolate Chunk Hazelnut Cake with Raspberry Sauce and
        Whipped Cream, 100–101

Fallen Chocolate Soufflé Cake, 154–55
Hazelnut and Almond Cake with Macerated Berries and
    Whipped Cream, 28–29
Orange Chiffon Cake with Lemon Verbena Custard and Berry
    Compote, 94–96
Torta de Tres Leches, 83–84
Capsouto, Jacques, Samuel, and Albert, 15, 30, 144
Capsouto Frères, 15, 30–35, 144–50
Carrot Soup with Cilantro, Cold Curried, 97
Caviar, Blue Potatoes with Crème Fraîche and, 109–10
Cerina, Guy, 21
Chanterelle, 15–16, 68–71, 151–55
Cheese
    Cheese Straws, 104
    Fennel and Parmigiano Salad, 140
    Portobello and Oyster Mushrooms with Herbed Goats' Milk
        Cheese in Puff Pastry, 57–58
    Roasted Sourdough Bread with Goats' Milk Cheese, Red
        Peppers, Basil and Black Olive Tapenade, 156–57
    Sautéed Radicchio with Melted *Taleggio* and Fontina Cheeses,
        135–36
    Warm Goats' Milk Cheese in Phyllo with Roasted Beets,
        112–13
Chicken
    Chicken Stock, 167
    Grilled Chicken Breasts with Oregano Butter, Warm Wild
        Rice Salad and Sautéed Mustard Greens, 58–61
    Grilled Chicken Salad with Thai Dressing, 39
    Moroccan Chicken Wrapped in Phyllo with a Roasted Pepper
        Dipping Sauce, 105–7
    Roasted Chicken with Oregano Bruschetta Stuffing, 114
    Sauté of Chicken with Parsley, Tomato and Garlic, 69–70
    Yucatán Grilled Chicken Breasts, 80
Chiodo, Alfred A., 17, 73, 112
Chocolate
    Chocolate Chunk Hazelnut Cake with Raspberry Sauce and
        Whipped Cream, 100–101
    Fallen Chocolate Soufflé Cake, 154–55
    Hot and Cold Chocolate Truffle Torte with Raspberry Purée,
        126–27
Cleaver, Mary, 16–17
Cleaver Company, The, 16–17, 36–42, 104–11
Corn
    Barbecued Breast of Duck with Sweet Corn Succotash, 92–93
    Corn Custard, 70
    Savory Corn Madeleines, 41
Crab
    Pan-Fried Soft-Shell Crabs with Tomato Vinaigrette and Fava
        Beans with Shallots and Summer Savory, 44–46
    Salad of Maine Crab with Hearts of Palm, 68
    Sauté of Soft-Shell Crabs with Wilted Spinach and Warm
        Summer Tomato Vinaigrette, 91–92
Cranberry Pudding, Steamed, 158–59
Crème Fraîche, 165

Dagorn, Roger, 16, 68, 151
De Niro, Robert, 20
Desserts
    Apple Tart, 138–39
    Black Mission Fig Soufflés with Walnut Crème Anglaise,
        148–50
    Chocolate Chunk Hazelnut Cake with Raspberry Sauce and
        Whipped Cream, 100–101
    Fallen Chocolate Soufflé Cake, 154–55
    Hazelnut and Almond Cake with Macerated Berries and
        Whipped Cream, 28–29
    Hot and Cold Chocolate Truffle Torte with Raspberry Purée,
        126–27
    Napoleon of Strawberries and Sweet Yogurt, 47
    Orange Chiffon Cake with Lemon Verbena Custard and Berry
        Compote, 94–96
    Orange Crème Brûlée, 61
    Pear Turnovers, 164
    Plum Clafouti, 71
    Plum Financier with Peach Purée, 89
    Poached Pears with Zabaglione Cream, 143
    Quince Fritters with Cider Caramel and Walnut Brittle Ice
        Cream, 116–17
    Raspberry Almond Tart, 131
    Steamed Cranberry Pudding, 158–59
    Strawberry Bread Pudding, 42
    Strawberry Ginger Rhubarb Crisp, 34–35
    Torta de Tres Leches, 83–84
    Warm Apple Empanadas with Orange Hibiscus Sauce, 121–22
    Warm Cashew Financier with Frozen Mascarpone Mousse,
        Coffee Anglaise, Chocolate Sauce and Candied Cashews,
        54–56
    White Peaches with Proseco, 67
    White Peach Granita with Raspberries, Zabaglione and Almond
        Biscotti, 76–77
Duane Park Cafe, 17, 73–77, 112–17
Duck, Barbecued Breast of, with Sweet Corn Succotash, 92–93

El Teddy's, 17–18, 78–84, 118–22
Emerman, Daniel, 15, 24, 140
Empanadas, Warm Apple, with Orange Hibiscus Sauce, 121–22
Endive with Roquefort and Walnuts, 108

Fallen Chocolate Soufflé Cake, 154–55
Fennel and Parmigiano Salad, 140
Fettucine with Rabbit, Squab and Black Olives, 140–42
Fig Soufflés, Black Mission, with Walnut Crème Anglaise, 148–50
Fish
    Broiled Salmon with Braised Escarole and Fried Leek Garnish, 98
    Fish Stock, 168
    Grilled Striped Bass with Chanterelles and Haricots Verts, 130–31
    Hazelnut-Crusted Fillet of Red Snapper with Cardamom Bercy
        Sauce, 33–34
    Paillard of Salmon in Fresh Laurier Vinaigrette with Leeks,
        Tomatoes and Asparagus, 49–52
    Salmon with Lentils and Red Wine Sauce, 124–25
    Seared Tuna with Spinach, White Beans and Lime-Marjoram
        Vinaigrette, 157–58

Smoked Salmon Rillettes, 30
Swordfish with Rosemary Polenta, Tomatoes and Fresh Herbs,
    87–88
Vitello Tonnato, 66–67
Yucatán Grilled Steak, Chicken and Whole Red Snapper, 80
Foie Gras, Sauté of, with Parsnips and Sweet and Sour Cherries,
    48–49
Frankel, Steve, 19

Garlic, roasting, 166
Gesualdi, Chris, 18
Gordon, David, 48, 90

Harding, Alan, 19, 43, 44, 156, 157
Hazelnut and Almond Cake with Macerated Berries and Whipped
    Cream, 28–29
Hazelnut-Crusted Fillet of Red Snapper with Cardamom Bercy
    Sauce, 33–34

Ice Cream, Walnut Brittle, and Quince Fritters with Cider Caramel,
    116–17

Johnnes, Daniel, 18, 85, 123

Klein, Peter, 18, 78, 118, 121

Lamb
    Grilled Lamb Shanks with Preserved Lemons on Arugula,
        162–63
    Roast Rack of Lamb, 26–27
Lemons, Preserved, 165–66
Lentils and Red Wine Sauce, Salmon with, 124–25
Lyle, Stephen, 20, 128, 130, 160, 162, 164
Lyness, Judy, 18

Maeda, Seiji, 17, 75
Magaritas, 78
McKirday, George, 20–21, 54
McNally, Brian and Keith, 19
Mendez, Ramiro, 18
Montrachet, 18–19, 85–89, 123–27
Moroccan Chicken Wrapped in Phyllo with a Roasted Pepper
    Dipping Sauce, 105–7
Mushrooms
    Asparagus, Morels, Ramps and Fiddlehead Ferns with Orange
        Oil and Edible Flowers, 36–37
    Beef with Black Trumpet Mushrooms, 151–153
    Braised Sweetbreads with Madeira and Wild Mushrooms, 146–48
    Grilled Portobello Mushrooms with Balsamic Vinaigrette, 32
    Grilled Striped Bass with Chanterelles and Haricots Verts, 130–31
    Portobello and Oyster Mushrooms with Herbed Goats' Milk
        Cheese in Puff Pastry, 57–58
    Potato Salad with Mushrooms and Sun-Dried Tomatoes, 75–76
    Squab with Young Morels, Roast Garlic and Sage Polenta,
        52–54
    Wild Mushroom and Huitlacoche Quesadillas with Mixed Greens,
        120
Mussels with Lime and Basil, 151

Nantucket Bay Scallops with Melted Leeks and Basil, 144–146
Napoleon of Strawberries and Sweet Yogurt, 47
Neiporent, Drew, 18, 20
Nosmo King, 19, 43–47, 156–59

Octopus and Squid Salad, Marinated, with Sherry Vinaigrette,
    Mango and Red Onion, 85–87
Odeon, The, 19–20, 128–31, 160–64
Oliva, Tom, 57, 97
Olive Breadsticks, 40
Orange Chiffon Cake with Lemon Verbena Custard and Berry
    Compote, 94–96
Orange Crème Brûlée, 61
Orzo with Lemon Thyme Zucchini Broth, 98–100
Osso Buco with Saffron Risotto, 136–38
Oysters
    Oysters in Champagne Sauce, 108–9
    Pan Roast of Oysters with Poblano Chiles on Toasted
        Cornbread, 160–62

Paillard of Salmon in Fresh Laurier Vinaigrette with Leeks,
    Tomatoes and Asparagus, 49–52
Pancakes, White Creamer Potato, with Herbs and Goats' Milk
    Cheese, 153–54
Panzanella with Mixed Field Greens, 73–74
Pasta
    Fettucine with Rabbit, Squab and Black Olives, 140–42
    Orzo with Lemon Thyme Zucchini Broth, 98–100
    Pasta Fagioli, 134–35
    Pasta with Sautéed Greens and Roasted Garlic, 38
Peaches
    Plum *Financier* with Peach Purée, 89
    White Peaches with Proseco, 67
    White Peach Granita with Raspberries, Zabaglione and Almond
        Biscotti, 76–77
Pears
    Pear Turnovers, 164
    Poached Pears with Zabaglione Cream, 143
Peppers
    roasting, 166
    Turban Squash and Ancho Chile Soup, 118
Pico de Gallo, 81–82
Pintabona, Don, 20, 90
Plates, warmed, 166
Plum *Clafouti*, 71
Plum *Financier* with Peach Purée, 89
Poached Pears with Zabaglione Cream, 143
Polenta
    Squab with Young Morels, Roast Garlic and Sage Polenta,
        52–54
    Swordfish with Rosemary Polenta, Tomatoes and Fresh Herbs,
        87–88
Portobello and Oyster Mushrooms with Herbed Goats' Milk
    Cheese in Puff Pastry, 57–58
Potatoes
    Blue Potatoes with Crème Fraîche and Caviar, 109–10
    Potato Salad with Mushrooms and Sun-Dried Tomatoes,
        75–76

Roasted Potatoes with Fresh Sage and Rosemary, 27–28
    White Creamer Potato Pancakes with Herbs and Goats' Milk
        Cheese, 153–54
Prosperi, Alessandro, 14–15, 28, 140
Puddings
    Steamed Cranberry Pudding, 158–59
    Strawberry Bread Pudding, 42
Pulito, Leo, 14, 64, 66, 134, 136

Quail Salad, Grilled, with Balsamic Vinaigrette, 123–24
Quesadillas, Wild Mushroom and *Huitlacoche*, with Mixed Greens,
    120
Quince Fritters with Cider Caramel and Walnut Brittle Ice Cream,
    116–17

Rabbit, Squab and Black Olives, Fettucine with, 140–42
Radicchio, Sautéed, with Melted *Taleggio* and Fontina Cheeses,
    135–36
Raspberries
    Chocolate Chunk Hazelnut Cake with Raspberry Sauce and
        Whipped Cream, 100–101
    Hot and Cold Chocolate Truffle Torte with Raspberry Purée,
        126–27
    Raspberry Almond Tart, 131
    White Peach Granita with Raspberries, Zabaglione and
        Almond Biscotti, 76–77
Ratatouille Tartlets, 110–11
Rhubarb Crisp, Strawberry Ginger, 34–35
Rice
    Arroz Verde, 83
    Osso Buco with Saffron Risotto, 136–38
    Saffron Risotto Cakes with Cheese and Vegetable Relish, 64,
        66
Rosenthal Wine Merchant, 36, 104

Saffron Risotto Cakes with Cheese and Vegetable Relish, 64, 66
Salads
    Fennel and Parmigiano Salad, 140
    Grilled Chicken Salad with Thai Dressing, 39
    Grilled Quail Salad with Balsamic Vinaigrette, 123–24
    Marinated Squid and Octopus Salad with Sherry Vinaigrette,
        Mango and Red Onion, 85–87
    Panzanella with Mixed Field Greens, 73–74
    Potato Salad with Mushrooms and Sun-Dried Tomatoes,
        75–76
    Salad of Maine Crab with Hearts of Palm, 68
    Warm Chicory Salad with Sweet Garlic, Croutons, Bacon and
        Roquefort Cheese, 128–29
    Warm Shrimp and Bean Salad, 24–26
Salmon
    Broiled Salmon with Braised Escarole and Fried Leek Garnish,
        98
    Paillard of Salmon in Fresh Laurier Vinaigrette with Leeks,
        Tomatoes and Asparagus, 49–52
    Salmon with Lentils and Red Wine Sauce, 124–25
    Smoked Salmon Rillettes, 30
Salsa Picante, 81–82

Sauces
    Avocado Sauce, 81–82
    Pico de Gallo, 81–82
    Salsa Picante, 81–82
Scallops, Nantucket Bay, with Melted Leeks and Basil, 144, 146
Seafood. *See also* Fish
    Marinated Squid and Octopus Salad with Sherry Vinaigrette,
        Mango and Red Onion, 85–87
    Mussels with Lime and Basil, 151
    Nantucket Bay Scallops with Melted Leeks and Basil,
        144–146
    Oysters in Champagne Sauce, 108–9
    Pan-Fried Soft-Shell Crabs with Tomato Vinaigrette and Fava
        Beans with Shallots and Summer Savory, 44–46
    Pan Roast of Oysters with Poblano Chiles on Toasted
        Cornbread, 160–62
    Sauté of Soft-Shell Crabs with Wilted Spinach and Warm
        Summer Tomato Vinaigrette, 91–92
    Tea-Smoked Shrimp Wrapped in Spinach, 111
    Tostadas de Camarónes, 78–79
    Warm Shrimp and Bean Salad, 24–26
Shrimp
    Tea-Smoked Shrimp Wrapped in Spinach, 111
    Tostadas de Camarónes, 78–79
    Warm Shrimp and Bean Salad, 24–26
Smoked Salmon Rillettes, 30
Soufflés, Black Mission Fig, with Walnut Crème Anglaise, 148–50
Soups
    Cold Curried Carrot Soup with Cilantro, 97
    Fresh Fava Bean and Asparagus Soup, 90
    Pasta Fagioli, 134–35
    Turban Squash and Ancho Chile Soup, 118
Sources, 169–72
Spinach
    Sauté of Soft-Shell Crabs with Wilted Spinach and Warm
        Summer Tomato Vinaigrette, 91–92
    Seared Tuna with Spinach, White Beans and Lime-Marjoram
        Vinaigrette, 157–58
    Tea-Smoked Shrimp Wrapped in Spinach, 111
Spoonbread, Spiced, 94
Squab
    Fettucine with Rabbit, Squab and Black Olives, 140–42
    Squab with Young Morels, Roast Garlic and Sage Polenta,
        52–54
Squash, Turban, and Ancho Chile Soup, 118
Squid and Octopus Salad, Marinated, with Sherry Vinaigrette,
        Mango and Red Onion, 85–87
Stocks, 167–68
Strawberries
    Napoleon of Strawberries and Sweet Yogurt, 47
    Strawberry Bread Pudding, 42
    Strawberry Ginger Rhubarb Crisp, 34–35
Sweetbreads, Braised, with Madeira and Wild Mushrooms,
        146–48
Swordfish with Rosemary Polenta, Tomatoes and Fresh Herbs,
        87–88

Tarts and tartlets
    Apple Tart, 138–39
    Raspberry Almond Tart, 131
    Ratatouille Tartlets, 110–11
Tea-Smoked Shrimp Wrapped in Spinach, 111
Tomatoes
    Oven-Dried Tomatoes, 115
    Potato Salad with Mushrooms and Sun-Dried Tomatoes,
        75–76
    Swordfish with Rosemary Polenta, Tomatoes and Fresh Herbs,
        87–88
Torta de Tres Leches, 83–84
Tostadas de Camarónes, 78–79
TriBeCa, history of, 10–11
Tribeca Grill, 20–21, 48–56, 90–96
Tuna
    Seared Tuna with Spinach, White Beans and Lime-Marjoram
        Vinaigrette, 157–58
    Vitello Tonnato, 66–67
Turban Squash and Ancho Chile Soup, 118
Turnovers, Pear, 164
Tutino, Charles, 15, 34, 146
Two Eleven Restaurant, 21, 57–61, 97–101

Vanilla sugar, 42
Veal
    Osso Buco with Saffron Risotto, 136–38
    Veal *Glace*, 168
    Veal Stock, 168
    Veal with Sweet Vermouth, Sage and Prosciutto, 74–75
    Vitello Tonnato, 66–67
Vegetables, sweating, 166
Vitello Tonnato, 66–67

Wagenknecht, Lynn, 19
Walnut Brittle Ice Cream, 116–17
Waltuck, David, 15–16, 68, 69, 151
Waltuck, Karen, 15–16
Washington Market, 10
Water bath, 166
White Creamer Potato Pancakes with Herbs and Goats' Milk
        Cheese, 153–54
White Peaches with Proseco, 67
White Peach Granita with Raspberries, Zabaglione and Almond
        Biscotti, 76–77
Wild Mushroom and *Huitlacoche* Quesadillas with Mixed Greens,
        120

Yucatán Grilled Steak, Chicken Breasts and Whole Red Snapper,
        80